Welcome

Remember the big 3-0? What about the 4-0, 5-0, and 6-0? All milestones. And all points when phrases such as "How did that happen?," "Where did the years go?," and "I'm so ancient" might have sprung to mind.

When you look back, however, 30 wasn't ancient. And neither's 60. The perception of age, like so many things, is relative. In this senior-focused special edition of *Breathe*, we see it is experienced and viewed differently across societies and cultures and that while there are always people out there who are younger than you, there'll be others who've clocked up many more years than you have.

In many respects, age—or, at least, getting older—is only as significant as you allow it to be. This is, perhaps, especially true when the "R" word begins to feature more frequently in one's vocabulary. Yes, retirement. Many embrace it, but for some it equals a crisis in self-confidence and anxiety about how the days, weeks, and months will pan out in future.

Who are you if no longer a teacher, retail assistant, or business analyst? Well, many things actually—the embodiment of years of knowledge, experiences, and emotions. You're still you. And what are you going to do now you no longer have to go into the school, boutique, or office every day? Well, lots! The question could, in fact, be "How will you be able to fit everything in while fulfilling family responsibilities?".

Life after full-time work or years dedicated to family life can be daunting, but think of the opportunities. Imagine having the time to study a much-loved subject at degree level; to visit art galleries when the hordes have passed; to pursue a long-held passion; to enjoy an unhurried coffee and some people-watching with a friend; to revisit far-flung countries whose riches you could only glance through a bus window on a two-week break from work; to sit and read a book from cover to cover. Imagine, finally, having time to care for your own needs and desires.

Whatever your age, set your own boundaries, follow your own style, do your own thing. Family and friends might raise an eyebrow, but who cares? It's your time—and *Senior Breathe* is ready to help you embrace it.

Contents

Design: Jo Chapman. **Editorial**: Susie Duff, Catherine Kielthy, Jane Roe. **Publisher**: Jonathan Grogan. **Cover illustration:** Lylean Lee.
Produced by Guild of Master Craftsman Publications Ltd. 86 High Street, Lewes, BN7 1XN, United Kingdom.

New beginning

Does the thought of retirement fill you with unbridled glee or a sense of unease? For some, it represents complete freedom—a time to take that longed-for round-the-world trip, for example—but for others, it can trigger bigger, trickier questions about identity and their place in the world. If you fall into the latter camp, perhaps it's time to take a leaf out of UK author Celia Dodd's inspiring book

Celia Dodd had come to a challenging crossroads in her life. After three decades as an in-demand journalist based in London, England, worryingly, the time between commissions seemed to be stretching out. Although only in her late 50s, she found herself questioning whether an early retirement might be on the cards. It was a subject very much on the agenda when she spent time with her friends, too. "In the same way that we all talked about parenthood when we were having children, retirement was the main topic of discussion," shares Celia, now 65 and a mother of three grown-up children.

But while many of her friends were anxious about this next stage of life, Celia started to think about another way of approaching it. She had watched her father fall into a deep depression when faced with his own retirement, a situation that made her more determined to enjoy a better experience. What followed was a period of self-reflection, where Celia took time to examine who she was in the absence of the work that had so defined her for most of her adult life, something many facing retirement will possibly face, too.

"It's perhaps one of the biggest transitions we go through," Celia says. "I found it helpful to see it for what it was—a crisis—because it really shakes things up. What are your core values, and what is important to you beyond work and being paid?"

For some, that question can prove hard to answer. While the routine of work may not always be 100 percent enjoyable, it does offer a reassuring structure and a place where many people create an identity—an identity that is deeply entwined with their sense of self-worth. Owen, one of the contributors in Celia's recently published

book, *Not Fade Away: How To Thrive In Retirement*, sums this up perfectly, saying: "Throughout my life, work has been the one single thing that has kept me going through all sorts of ups and downs."

Celia's first instinct? To test the waters and take on a new challenge. She decided to learn to play her flute in a different way. A classical flautist, she had always played from sheet music. Instead she joined a ceilidh band where she would have to play by ear. And being thrown so far out of her comfort zone brought an unexpected breakthrough, or as Celia recalls: "It was a real eye-opener. It broadened my life in so many unexpected ways. Yes, it was about new friendships and connections, but the most surprising thing? The energy it brought and how it made me feel better about life again. Our little ceilidh band won't sell out arenas, but the act of taking part gave me a sense of purpose—and ambition."

Finding a new purpose in life is perhaps at the heart of the struggle for those facing retirement. Pioneering psychologist Charlotte Bühler emphasized that goals hold the key to a healthy emotional life. Research seems to back this up: One study suggests that a strong sense of purpose "appears to lower the risk of dementia 2.4 times" and, even more powerfully, others claim that people with clear goals live longer than those without.

And it was Celia's own renewed sense of purpose that sparked the idea for *Not Fade Away*. With aging populations increasing globally, the book provides tips and inspiration for how to live your best retirement.

Not Fade Away features the experiences of some 60 people—drawn from every walk of life—who are busy navigating the road to, and through, retirement. Celia admits that the book is "relentlessly positive" and a conscious response to the negativity that can surround retirement and aging. She even confesses that her own husband thought it might be "challenging" to some readers not prepared for Celia's steely commitment to look on the bright side.

But Celia says her motives were not entirely selfless: "All of the advice in the book really applies to me, too. I'm the kind of person who would love to lie on the couch, watching box sets, knitting, and eating chocolate."

Chapters include some of the subjects already touched upon, such as *Preparing*, *Leaving Work Behind*, and *Finding New Purpose*. Backpacker Granny, real name Geraldine Forster, is one of the retirees blazing a trail in a new direction, for example.

The 74-year-old admits to being "terrified" when she embarked on her first solo trip to Bangkok, but she found a way to push through that fear. Today, she writes a blog and captures the destinations she visits through beautiful photography. Even more remarkably, it's all done on a shoestring—this intrepid woman stays in budget hostels.

While Backpacker Granny is possibly the exception rather than the rule, she highlights a key aspect of continuing to push boundaries. There are rewards to be enjoyed for those who continue to take chances.

"You are never too old to set another goal or to dream a new dream"

C.S. LEWIS

Mindful approach

Perhaps one of the most important themes at the heart of Celia's book is how people have managed the conflicting emotions they can feel on any given day. The new and unchartered territory of retirement can bring with it feelings of both happiness and anxiety. One of the touchstones in *Not Fade Away* for helping to deal with this is mindfulness. Reams of research into the health benefits of meditation—one form of mindfulness—has found evidence of a wealth of positive outcomes. These include a decrease in anxiety and depression, boosted self-esteem, increased restfulness and alertness, plus improved immune functioning and lower blood pressure. Surely all the encouragement you need to get your "Zen" on?

Practicing mindfulness can also help nurture a crucial space of stillness. When you find yourself caught on a rollercoaster of emotions, it can be easy to make hasty decisions, instead of taking time to really consider which direction to go in. Quietening the chatter of your mind can help those good ideas to bubble up to the surface.

Physical health is also of prime importance, of course, and many of the people Celia interviewed said they actually felt healthier in retirement, despite being older. One reason for this is having the luxury of time to find the kind of exercise you really enjoy.

Research suggests physical exercise not only gives your body a workout, but the endorphins released also lift your mood. It can be something as simple as a daily walk in the park and taking the opportunity to fill your lungs with fresh air.

Of course, mindfulness and keeping active aren't going to pay the bills—but they are an important foundation. Practical matters are addressed in the book in the chapters *Money*, *Home: Moving, Downsizing, Staying Put*, and *Living Alone*.

But perhaps the final word about living your best retirement should go to Celia, who reached this conclusion: "Retirement, like any life change, prompts soul-searching, reflection, and personal growth. You stop caring so much about what other people think, and there's a new freedom in that. It's about accepting the change: You've got life skills and valuable experience, and this is the time to harvest them."

Not Fade Away: How To Thrive In Retirement, Celia Dodd, Green Tree, £12.99.

CELIA'S TOP FIVE TIPS FOR LIVING YOUR BEST RETIREMENT

Prepare

"It's better to start creating the kind of life you want before it happens. So, start building new social interests and networks—it will act as a bridge into the next phase. They will act as the constant things in your life, which can be very supportive and reassuring when everything else is changing."

Aim for contrast

"Mix things up between relaxing and doing something quite demanding. We all know that feeling at work when you do something you find challenging and the sense of achievement you feel afterward. Yes, I love lying on the couch, knitting, and eating chocolate, but I enjoy it more knowing I've done something more productive before."

Have new things to talk about

"If you're constantly saying, 'I used to do this' or 'I used to do that,' it puts the conversation in the past. It's much better to be able to say, 'I'm doing a photography course' or 'I'm volunteering at the local church.' Other people will then feed off that and the conversation is much more upbeat."

Keep a diary

"Keeping a record of your achievements—small and big—can be a good reminder of how far you've come. Also write lists of the things you still aim to achieve."

Practice patience

"Embrace the process of creating your new identity and accept that it takes time. But be proactive: Create new rituals to help shape this new phase of life."

Don't stop believing

It's an assumption, sadly often universally acknowledged, that when you reach a certain age, life takes a turn for the worse. But, of course, you know better

Let's pretend to play *Family Feud*. If you're not familiar with the TV game show, 100 members of the public are asked a question and contestants have to guess the top answers. So, how do you think people will respond to: "Describe someone who's aged 60 or above"? Inspiring? Motivational? Having a lust for life? It would be refreshing if these words appeared on the list. The chances are, though, that more derogatory terms—dull, wrinkly, over the hill—are the standout survey results.

It's staggering how negative preconceptions about older adults are so prevalent in society, and much of the population resort to easy stereotypes when put on the spot. Times are changing, though, and attitudes and social norms need to keep up. Rewind the clock back to the decade you were born, and, yes, many people saw retirement as that opportunity to slow down and enjoy a quiet, easy existence. Today, it's quite the opposite. Healthy and financially stable individuals are grabbing life by the horns and embracing their new-found freedom. They're discovering a thirst for knowledge, a desire for travel, and a yearning to maximize both their mental well-being and fitness levels. Take it easy? Not at all.

Be your true self

Of course, it's understandable that when you overhear cute remarks about how you should act, behave, or dress, you can be knocked sideways, but it's ageism that ought to be knocked out. Unwarranted assumptions and sweeping generalizations about baby boomers are not acceptable, just as no one should be of the opinion that all millennials are lazy and entitled.

Try to disentangle yourself from cynical comments, made without any real insight or consideration for others. You know what's true and what to believe, so dispel any bothersome doubt. Your peers, and probably you yourself, are proving every day that age is not a barrier. You can be powerful, sexy, successful, daring, gregarious, witty—the list doesn't have to end. Seek inspiration from friends and acquaintances, set your own expectations, and dare to be different from society's stifling views about seniors.

Age is irrelevant when it comes to fulfilling your dreams, and for many, their greatest achievements happen in later life. Gladys Burrill, who celebrated her 100th birthday last November, completed her first marathon when she was 86. Mother Teresa received the Nobel Peace Prize aged 69.

Dame Judi Dench, star of movies like *Mrs. Brown* and *Shakespeare In Love*, has had seven Oscar nominations, all of them after she turned 60. And, at 85, designer Karl Lagerfeld continues to push boundaries as the head of three leading fashion brands.

Trust your knowledge

As for older people being unaware of—or unable to grasp—the digital world, the reverse seems to be occurring. According to a Pew Research Center survey, around four-in-ten (42 percent) of American adults aged 65 and older now report owning smartphones, up from just 18 per cent in 2013. Internet use and home broadband adoption among this group have also risen substantially. Today, 67 percent of seniors use the internet—a 55-percentage-point increase in just under two decades. And for the first time, half of older Americans now have broadband at home. It doesn't follow that they'll all be able to debate the pros and cons of Google Pixel's Qualcomm Snapdragon 845 processor as they converse with teenage grandkids, but so what? How often has a younger relative called you up to ask how long a turkey should roast in the oven; whether it's a good time to plant allium bulbs, or how today's political climate compares to the fevered 1980s? Your knowledge and life experiences are not to be underrated, so relish what you do know—and share it with others.

That's exactly what Tricia Cusden, a retired management training consultant, is doing. As founder of Look Fabulous Forever (lookfabulousforever.com), she's sharing ways to embrace the benefits of aging. She's also challenging perceptions, and wasn't afraid of sharing her outrage when model Cara Delevingne, then 25, was revealed as the face of Dior's antiaging products.

It's up to everyone to make a stand, shift society's dated discriminations, and end ageism. People need to be judged on their own merits rather than for how long they've been on the planet. Know what's true and accept only that of which you have evidence. Life is amazing at any age. Don't allow anyone to convince you otherwise.

"I have no special talents. I am only passionately curious"

ALBERT EINSTEIN

Seize the day

Sometimes life can get in the way of pursuing your passions and following your dreams. But you can give yourself permission to do the things you've always longed to do

Think of something you've always wanted to do: Play Debussy's *Clair de Lune* on the piano, research and pen a biography of an inspiring playwright, tread the boards with the grace of Glenn Close. Now think of all the reasons that have meant you've never even taken the first step to get there: Exams to pass, parents to please, career ladders to climb, mortgages to pay, families to raise, older relatives and grandchildren to look after. The list goes on... and on. But perhaps it's time for the reasons to stop (that includes number one, the commonly shared, widely believed: "I can't do that") and for the road to achieving that long-held passion to start.

What's standing in your way?

In her international bestseller, *The Artist's Way, A Course In Discovering And Recovering Your Creative Self,* Julia Cameron states: "Give yourself permission to be a beginner. By being willing to be a bad artist, you have a chance to be an artist and perhaps, over time, a very good one. When I make this point in teaching, I am met by instant defensive hostility: 'But do you know how old I will be by the time I learn to really play the piano/act/paint/write a decent play?' Yes... the same age you will be if you don't."

Julia makes a valid point. You'll be the same age whether you start something immediately or not. Two years from now, wouldn't it be better to feel that you've made progress rather than still being in the same position of contemplation?

Sue Brown, an artist and stationery designer, was in her early 40s when she began to learn to play the piano. Her decision was prompted by a long-held interest in music—one her family had discouraged when she was a child—and a feisty aunt who had defied her own father's wishes that she take up a proper job and instead pursued a musical career. Sue's family had held similar views, hoping she would train as a doctor or an architect. "My aunt was a key influence on me wanting to play," says Sue. "She told me funny stories and had such a glamorous life. I was fascinated by her.

"She was still playing the piano in her 80s and 90s. My own interest had lain dormant because I hadn't had any opportunity and I thought how am I going to do this?"

The occasion arose when Sue's parents died in the same year. "Once I'd sorted everything with my brothers and dealt with some of my grief, I started to embark upon things my parents might not have approved of," she says. "For around two years, I began doing new things. I took up horse-riding but ached all over, started creative writing, art, singing, and a psychology degree."

For Sue, playing the piano was another passion that had been pushed under the surface. That changed when Sue took her children for piano lessons. "They weren't interested," she recalls, "but I was, and I asked the teacher if she taught adults. I thought: 'If I don't do this now, when am I going to do it? I can't keep putting off these things. Instead of being someone else's idea of me, I could actually be me.'"

Time for you

Sometimes it can be hard to give yourself permission to do things that bring you joy and happiness. It can also feel daunting to start something new, especially if you're at an age where you feel largely proficient and

confident in a lot of what you do. But stepping outside your comfort zone, however frightening, can bring with it plenty of benefits.

"I feel really glad that I started to play the piano," enthuses Sue. "I'm addicted to it and can easily lose two hours practicing. I gain a huge sense of pride when I can actually play a piece. I started at zero and now I'm at grade six level, which has given me such a massive confidence boost."

Time for friends

Starting a new passion project can also lead to new friendships and contacts. Sue joined a piano group, which enabled her to meet others who also enjoyed the instrument. "I wish I'd joined earlier," she says. "I realized other people make mistakes when playing and it has helped me to let go of some of my perfectionist tendencies. I know I'm going to get things wrong, but it doesn't matter. I need to stick with it and persevere. I also like the fact this is my choice. Nobody's pushing me to do it. I'm the one who wants to proceed and progress."

Finding a passion project might come easily. It's usually the thing that creates a small bubble of excitement and energy when you think about it. It could be when you pick up your camera and head out for the day or if you snap a great shot on your phone. You might feel it when you run your hands over brightly colored materials in a fabric store and start thinking about all the wonderful things you could make. Choose something you love and which, if possible, gets you into that magical "flow" state mentioned by creatives and performers, where you feel energized and time disappears.

After all, you're doing this for your own satisfaction. It's a chance to express your authentic self. There are no rules and there's no need to please others or seek financial gain. There's the opportunity to get in touch with your inner child, to play, to color outside the lines. Take up pottery and throw your own vases; note your inner dreams in a scrapbook; become a member of the local amateur dramatics group; write; draw; paint; take photos and share them on Instagram.

It's never too late

Having focus will help you achieve your goals, says Sue: "You realize it's your time, your money, and your effort and become more brutal about what you're prepared to accept. I didn't have time to waste, so I left a piano teacher who didn't suit me and agreed on how I wanted to proceed with another. I knew I wanted to learn theories and pieces that enabled me to progress, but I didn't want the pressure of exams."

And remember age is no barrier to your dreams. Samuel L. Jackson was 45 when he achieved his breakthrough success in 1994 movie *Pulp Fiction*; Irish writer Frank McCourt was 66 when *Angela's Ashes* was published; and Laura Ingalls Wilder, who penned the *Little House On The Prairie* series, published the first of eight books at age 65 and finished her final book aged 76. As British author and poet George Eliot once said: "It is never too late to be what you might have been."

STARTING A PASSION PROJECT

If you're keen to pursue a long-held interest or a new dream but aren't sure where to start, you might consider some of these questions:

What things did you love doing as a child? Did you have a favorite hobby that you've long forgotten about that you'd like to explore? Was there a story or painting that you once started and haven't returned to for years?

Do you follow certain people or subjects on Instagram or other social media platforms? Perhaps they could give you an insight into a project you'd like to try.

What books are you interested in when you go to a bookstore or library? Do these give you an insight into a passion?

Do you find yourself thinking: "I'd like to do that." If so, what's the first action you need to do to start?

Are you inspired by other people and their projects and skills? Are they doing something you'd love to do?

Who do you know that might help or support you with your passion (if you feel you need it)?

Where might you carry out your project? Could you turn a neglected room in your home into an artist's studio?

Go rogue

Throw out the rule book and unleash your inner rebel

Think about an act of personal rebellion. Not one from your teen years or 20s, but something relevant to the here and now. It might, as Jenny Joseph suggests in her poem, *Warning*, be wearing purple with a red hat and by spending money on brandy, summer gloves, and satin sandals, all of which sound appealing. Yet, is this what it's really like? Is it possible to be in touch with your inner rebel and to follow individual style choices in the face of societal norms about age-appropriate clothes and behaviors? The short answer... yes.

Every generation—and age group—faces rules about what counts as acceptable forms of dress. There's the school code; the office code; the moms' and dads' code; and, maybe now, the "at-your-age?" code. It's implicit in the hairdresser's suggestion that it's time to opt for a shorter cut and style (it will mask the gray more effectively) and it's there when a store assistant ushers you away from the floral halter-neck bikinis and toward the one-piece swimsuits (they'll cover excess flesh, scars, and any evidence of having lived on the planet for more than 20 years).

It goes on. Cover the tops of your arms; forget too-plunging, too-short, or too-tight; and don't imagine ever buying again any glamorous heels. After all, you're a "certain age." It's time to join the comfortable-shoe gang. Rules schmules! Maybe there's another way.

Thankfully, over the years, there's been a change in perspective. Now, grandmothers, mothers, and daughters are just as likely to be sharing clothing and attending the same yoga class, while men in their 50s, 60s, and beyond can be seen clad in selvedge denim and Dr. Martens.

All of this is great news, especially for those who want to do things differently, but feel hemmed in by societal norms. Seeing their peers dare to defy age-appropriate rules can help them to channel their own inner rebel, and to give themselves permission to express their true selves. Rise up and take the plunge. Creating a personal style has no age limitation, and rebellion—whether it be of a personal or political nature—isn't confined to the young. Age is no barrier to attending demonstrations, visiting far-flung climes, or wearing sleeveless dresses.

For some, of course, conforming to rules, towing the line, and pleasing others might be a natural and happy default position. For those less content with the situation, it could be time to make a change. Gina Pell, 49, is an internet entrepreneur who has created a new term for those who understand that age is not a limiting factor. Say hello to the perennial. "From childhood and beyond, perennials get involved," she explains. "They stay curious, mentor others, [they're] passionate, compassionate, creative, confident, collaborative, global-minded, [and] risk-takers."

I am lucky enough to have known someone who epitomized this attitude. Her name was Edith and we met back in the 1990s when I was living in New York. There was a 50-plus age-gap between us—I was in my early 30s, Edith was in her mid-80s. We used to hang out in restaurants and cafés where we'd discuss books, philosophy, and everyday life.

Edith had many friends her age who'd moved south to Florida. They would regularly call trying to encourage her to follow them to its sunny climes. Her response was always the same: "Why would I want to move there, it's full of old people?" She continued to live in the Big Apple until her death in her early 90s. She was a remarkable woman who stood up for what she believed in, had her own style, and certainly didn't follow the rules.

Some people appear to be born with this confidence and approach to life while others gain it through their experiences. Either way, it can be an advantage in later years when worries that might once have been considered important no longer matter and impressing others or listening to their judgment is not on the agenda.

Perhaps now's the time to set and follow your own rules. They can be as discreet or as indiscreet as suits your style. Whether that's growing your (gray or pink) hair long, leading a protest march, taking a solo trip to the movies, wearing glam heels, or pulling on the selvedge denim jeans, don't let fear of other people's perceptions hold you back. Beware, though, that once your inner rebel has been unleashed, it's unlikely he or she will want to go back in the box.

And what do you do?

Establishing a sense of identity outside the work arena can take some time, but it's worth putting in the effort to make it another positive step in your life

One of the most significant challenges of retirement can be making the adjustment from working nine-to-five or regularly commuting—anything that constitutes a particular daily and weekly routine—to suddenly being in charge of your own time... a lot of it. And it's not just the lack of structure that can pose a challenge, but also a perceived change in identity.

An accepted part of Western social interaction lies in asking what someone does when you first meet them. It's possible, of course, given the way the gig economy is swiftly progressing, that in the future this will die out when the answer consists of a long list of various jobs and contracts. "...so that's Monday. On Tuesday morning I do some legal work for a cooperative, and later I do a barista shift." For now, however, it's a given that "what do you do?" is a frequently asked question.

If you're retired, especially recently, are you happy to say just that and leave it there? You might prefer to say "I'm a retired accountant" or "well, I was an accountant." That's fine, and will quite often be relevant to a conversation, but surely time is too precious to spend it living in the past and talking about what you used to do? Especially if, after leaving full-time work, you find yourself doing something that gives you as much, if not more, satisfaction than your previous job, be it a hobby, volunteering, or spending extra time with loved ones.

Level playing field

People have different experiences of retirement, just as people have different experiences in other stages of life. But there are some perceptions about it that have negative connotations, which you don't have to buy into, and they can be challenged. "You feel you are all lumped together," says Eileen Murphy, who retired from her job as director of hospitality services at the University of Central Lancashire, aged 60. "You might be a captain of industry one day, and the next you've retired and you're just 'an old-age pensioner.' There's a terrific leveling once you retire." Eileen, now 76, may be all too aware of the negative perception, but that's all it is—a perception, and not a fact of life. She left work and never looked back, and has packed a lot into retirement so far, including a full-time four-year degree, regular voluntary work as treasurer for an opera and ballet society, and a major move to be nearer family.

"I never missed work for a second," says Eileen, "and yet I was really keen on my career. Throughout my working life it was massively important. And you just walk away from it and shrug your shoulders, you know—it's finished."

Eileen's attitude to leaving work is a healthy one, but a genuine feeling of retirement grief isn't uncommon among others. If you've had a specific role at work, it can be difficult to adapt to losing it—it may have been a position of authority, as a manager, or you may have had a pastoral role and miss being able to help people. Others may be left feeling bereft by the disappearance of a structured working week or relationships with colleagues. If you aren't prepared for this, it can knock your confidence and render you directionless.

"I must admit I'd always dreaded retirement," says Kim Smith, who left her role as a journalist in 2017, aged 59. "Firstly, because I'd always loved my job and secondly, because I hated the thought of losing direction in life. However, changes at work meant that the creative input in my job disappeared and I began to dread going in. When the chance of redundancy came along I grabbed it and forced myself to adjust my mindset about giving up work, beginning to look at it as a fresh start—that's the only way to cope with it.

"It's a poor metaphor, but it feels like you're driving in the fast lane and suddenly somebody slams on the brakes. It's a difficult mindset to adjust to. It's about self-worth and, with retirement, you can suddenly find yourself floundering. It's not about self-importance, it really is just feeling that you've got something to aim for."

Kim had guessed that she would struggle at first, so took steps to find volunteer work that she knew she would enjoy and to which she felt she could meaningfully contribute. She also joined a local French conversation class, a genealogy group, a walking group, and keeps her fitness levels up with gym classes and swimming.

Lost structures

"It's natural for anyone who works to fantasize about leaving behind the daily grind—no more alarm clocks or commuting, less pressure, endless free time," says Caroline Abrahams, director of an older people's charity. "However, while it may sound great to have a limitless choice, work gives a structure to the day and it can feel very strange when it is no longer there.

"Many people are unprepared for this once they retire and find they need to take some concrete steps to retain a sense of purpose and to avoid being bored or feeling down. Retirement should be a time of enjoyment and it can be, too, with a bit of thinking on your part." Caroline recommends volunteering and also reconnecting with hobbies once you have more time, plus learning new things, and taking on fresh challenges.

You may have felt constricted by routine while working, and it's great to find freedom from that. But most people welcome routine, however loose. Elizabeth Knight, who at 70 retired from the travel and hospitality business, says: "When you retire, you have to have structure. It's no good saying: 'I'll just sit and wait for things to fall in my lap.' I think you have to work at retirement as much as you had to work at your job.

"Each week I make sure I've got something on every day. I keep a diary and if there's an empty day the following week, then I fill it. When I left [work], I didn't realize how important that was. So I think the first six months of retirement are quite difficult. Adjusting to the fact you've got the whole day ahead of you, and you don't have to be at work by 9.00 a.m."

It is a massive lifestyle change and your feelings about it may be confused at first—perhaps missing a busy office atmosphere or finding it odd that there's no "cut-off" point that separates your work day from your own time. You can take advice, of course, but everyone's situation is different. If you're feeling lost because it seems you're suddenly on shifting sands, remember it's a common reaction. So don't compound any negative thoughts you may have by berating yourself for struggling with it.

Staying healthy is paramount, and in retirement you have more time to do this, whether it's walking your dog (looking after pets can provide structure, especially if it's taking the dog for a walk two or three times a day), swimming, yoga, or Pilates. And there are numerous mindfulness apps out there, such as Headspace, 10% Happier, Insight Timer, or Calm.

Freedom at last

Above all, try to treat any change in identity that comes about through retirement as the fresh start it is and endeavor to take full advantage of it. Even if your job left little time for hobbies, that doesn't mean you don't have any interests to pursue. Join some local groups. Visit art galleries. Go to concerts. Enrol at a gym. Start a book club with friends. You don't have to say "yes" to everything—you may feel you know at this stage in your life if you're going to be left cold by interpretive dance—but try some new things. Robert Delamontagne, a writer who has studied the psychological effects of retirement, has said it can be a time for personal growth, which can lead to greater freedom. And isn't it freedom that so many people desire during much of their working life?

Fit for life

Modern lifestyles can easily wreck one's health, which is why it's more important than ever to keep active. And the good news is there's no need to don Lycra and hotfoot it to a high-impact aerobics class (unless, of course, that's your thing)

Finding an enjoyable way to maintain your fitness levels is essential to everyone who wants to stay healthy, energetic, and independent. It's especially important as you get older, when levels of daily activity for most of the population dwindle.

Studies show that American adults aged over 60 spend around 60 percent of their waking time on average sitting or lying down every day. Far from being happy couch potatoes, though, studies show that there is a serious downside to inactivity, as it indicates a higher rate of falls, obesity, heart disease, and early death compared with the general population.

The great news is that remaining active reduces the risk of diseases such as diabetes, dementia, and arthritis and can stave off their progression if you find that you are affected. Muir Gray, a professor at Oxford University in the UK, points out: "It's much more important to be fit and healthy later in life—from our 60s onward—than in our 20s and 30s." An expert on how modern lifestyles can wreck one's health, Gray says there's no reason to put off getting in shape—whatever your age, ailments, or activity level, and that "it's never too late to start reaping the benefits." He suggests it's a good idea to talk to your doctor about what might work for you.

Francesca Farrell, a doctor in London, England, says: "I think age is just a number and should not dictate what exercise you can and can't do. But with all types of exercise a good warm-up before and a good stretch after is important, as is increasing intensity and duration gradually. Listening to your body is key."

Those with joint problems such as arthritis should avoid high-impact exercise like running, particularly on harder surfaces—sidewalks and Tarmac. Good footwear helps, she says, and suggests swimming for aerobic fitness and muscle strength without being high impact on joints; dancing for core strength, balance, and social interaction; tai chi, which is known to reduce risk of falls; Pilates for muscle and core tone; and yoga for strength of mind and improved flexibility. "The main thing is to find an exercise you enjoy and do it regularly," she says. "Maybe you can add cycling and walking into your everyday life. Get fit while saving the planet."

Someone who understands the importance of fitness for an older generation is Geoff Walcott. Geoff had worked in telecoms for almost 40 years when he retired, but six months afterward, he was, in his own words, "going nuts at home." He took a part-time job at his local health club, which led to him retraining as a personal

trainer. Geoff is a fine testament to a lifelong love of fitness: He had been a sports coach from his early years; he joined a running club in his 40s; and went on to compete in sprint races worldwide. In his new personal-trainer role he was soon working "seven days a week, out of choice"—coaching clients through fitness regimes. Now 66, he's especially mindful of tailoring fitness for older clients.

"I'm a realist. You do slow down with age," he says. "I feel the same as 20 years ago, and still do everything I did then, but I know I don't have unlimited energy. I don't try to compete with those half my age. It's about being the best I can be."

Martine Howard, 62, had been very active from her youth: She was a dancer in the 1970s with the television dance troupe the Young Generation, and sang in the pop group Guys 'n' Dolls. But by her early 50s, having raised her daughter, she was exercising less and her fitness level dropped. She began to suffer painful backache and sciatica. "It was horrible and I often found it hard to pull myself out of bed."

Then she tried zumba, the Latin-inspired dance and aerobics regime, and was hooked. She built up gradually and three months later found her back pain was gone. She loved it so much she trained, at 54, as a teacher of zumba. Along with stretch and ballroom-dancing inspired classes, she teaches eight local classes a week.

Like Geoff, Martine's lifelong love of fitness and health stood her in good stead. "For anyone who hasn't been very active and is just starting, I'd say don't start by running or doing anything to excess. They would benefit from expert guidance, be it in a class or one-to-one training." She acknowledges it's not easy for everyone. "People do get lazy and think: 'Can I be bothered? I'd rather sit here and have a glass of wine.' I can be the same, and I love my food, too. But I can't enjoy either if my body's not in great shape."

She teaches zumba gold (for 50-plus) and says: "Apart from being so much more toned within two or three months, a lot of my zumba students say they can't believe how much better they feel."

As someone who's gone through pain herself, she feels she can help those of all ages overcome similar problems. She admits her body has changed with age and she has slowed down, but sees this as giving her an edge over younger instructors.

"You can't help your skin getting wrinkly and things going south," she says. "But you can make yourself feel and look your best through exercise." And Martine is the living proof—she performed with the Dancing Nanas at the annual Royal Variety Performance. Martine doesn't look like a typical "nana." "I passionately believe that being fit keeps me young," she says.

Geoff agrees: "Being 66, I know it's not all about your age, it's about your attitude. My older clients often train harder than the younger ones. I've spent my entire life helping people achieve their exercise goals, and I'm very focused on helping everyone get better, whatever their age." So it seems staying fit and active doesn't have to involve running marathons or climbing mountains. Attaining fitness can be gentle and enjoyable, and when it can be incorporated into your daily life, you're more likely to stay with it.

Turn the page to discover the many ways of introducing fitness into your everyday routine.

"The main thing is to find an exercise you enjoy, and do it regularly"

FRANCESCA FARRELL

WAYS TO INTRODUCE EXERCISE INTO YOUR LIFE

Zumba gold
Zumba is known as the ultimate dance party, bringing together Latin-inspired moves and music with more traditional aerobic exercises. Zumba gold classes are set at a level and pace suitable for all ages and abilities—the best part is that classes are so much fun, it won't even feel like exercise.

Dance
Show off your moves at a dance class of your choice. More relaxed classes include everything from Latin to ballroom, freestyle to line dancing. Learning to dance and remembering footwork will help to support brain and memory functions.

Pilates and yoga
Pilates is all about slow, controlled movements to help build up your core muscle strength. Yoga concentrates on gentle stretching to boost your flexibility and balance. Most exercises are performed seated or lying down. In addition, you get some wonderful relaxation time at the end of most classes.

Seated exercise
Gentle, chair-based exercises are great for improving posture and balance and are suitable for people with reduced mobility. Some classes incorporate resistance bands (see below) and hand weights for muscle strengthening. Martine teaches chair-based zumba: "Moving your arms, legs, and torso, and anything that wants to move, to a funky beat, even while seated, is good for the body, mind, and soul."

Resistance bands
These strips or loops of stretchy material are a safe way to build muscle strength and improve flexibility. Alan Wells, 66, the 100m Olympic gold medalist in 1980, found he couldn't lift weights because of a long-term back problem, so turned to resistance bands instead. "They're a great alternative for building strength without lifting metal," he explains. With the right exercise they can sort out all sorts of injuries: "They even cured my golfer's shoulder," adds Alan.

Tai chi
Tai chi, which originates from Ancient China, is now practiced by people of all ages around the world. Focusing on slow and gentle movements, the practice supports balance and posture, and is known for its positive impact on mental well-being and as a way to relax and de-stress.

Walking clubs
Explore your local area and meet new people at an organized walking group. You may have a walk leader and groups go at a pace that suits everyone. Walks can be a mixture of flat walks through to more demanding, hillier trails over different distances. Walking really is one of the best forms of all-round exercise.

Walking soccer
Competitive, fast, and lots of fun, walking soccer is gaining popularity. You may be able to join a local team of players who want to continue playing the "beautiful game" and improve their general fitness.

Park and walk
You may need a car to get toward your destination, but you can also combine it with some walking activity too. Park some distance away from where you need to be and walk the rest.

Kris Akabusi, 59, a Commonwealth gold and Olympic silver medalist, says that when he's meeting a friend or going into town, he parks his car a mile away from where he needs to be: "I still get there but I get 20 minutes' exercise too."

Try something new
When it comes to exercise, it can be good to surprise your body, to keep it interesting. Sally Gunnell, who won the 400m hurdles gold medal at the 1992 Olympic Games, suggests trying swimming, cycling, Pilates, or a short run. "When the body faces something new, it has to work a little bit harder," she says. Sally also advises working on balance and coordination, which deteriorate with age—for this, cycling and low-impact exercise is good, as is tai chi, or even ballroom dancing.

The art of letting go

While it can be difficult to give up the habit of exerting control over every aspect of your life, adopting a more flexible approach and welcoming change can help to make for a more liberating, independent future

You've been asked on a date for the first time in 30 years and you're worried you'll have nothing to say. You've decided to downsize your house but don't know how to begin to search for a new home. You'd like to start life-drawing classes, but don't want your efforts to leave you looking foolish or out of your depth. That last scenario may sound insignificant compared to the first two situations, but if you're someone who likes certainty in their life, coping with the unknown can feel overwhelming and potentially debilitating, however big or small that change may be.

If the term "creature of habit" resonates with you, you may be someone who finds it hard to deal with change, who likes to feel in control, and the manager of your own destiny. But, what's the worst that could happen? At that precise moment a thousand images flash through your mind. You've already imagined the worst, the second worst, and almost every other possible scenario in between.

Maintaining control over the situation is paramount, not letting in room for unpredictability or undesirable outcomes. Are your anxiety levels going up even just thinking about it?

Resisting change

Fear of losing control is intangible—yet if you're someone who resists change, that fear can feel real. It plays to deep fears of the unknown and uncertainty. To some extent everyone will have experienced this dread from time to time. It's only human to feel anxious about starting a new job or concerned for the health of your children. But for some, living with the fear of losing control has a stranglehold over their lives that seems unbreakable.

Loss of any kind can be difficult to cope with. Often fear of not being in control occurs when a situation is forced upon you—a sudden unexpected illness or a problem within the family that leaves you reeling and reliant on others, unable to see a way forward.

Freedom in the unpredictable

Perhaps you have always regarded yourself as being the strong one, the confident one, the manager, parent, carer, or friend who always knows just what to do and how the story will end. Your control was exactly what kept your ship afloat for so long, but now it threatens to sink you, overwhelming you with an anxiety that will take you down with it.

Facing situations where the outcome is unknown and where, despite your best efforts, you can't affect the results, can be terrifying. And yet, it is precisely where freedom lies.

Freedom from having to be the one who always has the answers, from being the one shouldering the burdens of others and the one who has to make every decision.

True autonomy

Letting go of control is not about losing yourself, your dreams, or autonomy. It is about facing up to the unknown with the confidence that, while you're not in charge of the situation, you are in charge of yourself and your responses to it.

The problem lies with the pull between the desire for control and the reality of living in an uncertain world. These two positions jostle for power, creating stress and anxiety. Loosening your normally tight grip on maintaining a sense of equilibrium may bring about emotional benefits, but is this something that's easier said than done?

Those who experience high levels of anxiety over losing control are often regarded as perfectionists—the type of people who enjoy order, structure, and certainty in their lives. Understandably, if you're someone who clings on to control, the potential for change can be challenging. Ironically, it's possible that the desire for certainty may have hindered you throughout life, but there will be a deep-rooted resistance against operating in any other way.

Seizing a different kind of power, however, will give you the opportunity to let go. Realizing the futility of hanging on to control of situations and people and instead saying: "I will not worry about actions outside my control, I will concentrate on dealing with my own reactions to them," is the power that comes from within.

Furthermore, it's time to drop any negative labels you give yourself as a worrier. Breaking free of self-administered restrictions to your identity is tough after a lifetime of believing it, but writing yourself a new story is never too late. If fear of facing an uncertain future plays a big part in your anxiety, then practicing courage is the antidote. However, demonstrating courage requires some practice, perhaps more than you thought possible.

Dealing with the anxiety of losing control is a fantastic first step. It's worth remembering that if you have an anxious mind you may struggle to process thoughts rationally and find it hard to make decisions.

Ironically, one of the better ways for dealing with anxiety is to avoid trying to control and submerge it, but instead to let your anxiety come to the fore and face it head on. Giving your worrying thoughts a name and speaking out loud about your tumble of emotions and feelings around a situation will help to give anxiety a sense of proportion. From there it becomes a matter of breaking the habit of feeling anxious into bite-sized pieces and slowly realizing that you are not, in fact, losing control, but gaining it with every forward step you take.

Practicing a guided muscle relaxation, following certain mindfulness techniques, and simply taking the time to talk through your worries and the process of dealing with these fears and anxieties, will put you on the path toward a freedom that comes from letting go. Letting go of control, and the fear of losing control, and moving toward a happier, less anxious time of life. Liberate yourself and feel free.

STEP-BY-STEP GUIDE TO LOSING CONTROL WITHOUT FEAR

- **Admit** you need to bring about change in your life and that you struggle with feelings of fear.
- **Talk** to a trusted friend, family member, or therapist about your situation and make yourself accountable to them.
- **Set goals** and make them achievable within a realistic time frame.
- **Face** your anxiety and give it a name.
- **Practice** techniques that help you to feel relaxed and calm, and enable you to think more clearly about your situation.

Revolutionize the weekend

Have your weekends become too busy for you to relax? Structure in two consecutive days during the week to enjoy well-earned downtime

You dream about it for years, imagining the days in the future when you're no longer working nine-to-five, Monday to Friday, and every day feels like the weekend. But when that time finally arrives, the reality can be different. Instead of having all seven days to yourself, you rarely get two, particularly two consecutively. They seem to blend into one long stretch and suddenly weeks pass, months too, and you realize you haven't had a proper rest in ages—a couple of consecutive days where you can properly unwind. Does this sound familiar? If so, you might want to start making plans to reclaim an old-fashioned two-day weekend.

It doesn't matter if, because of new commitments, you can't take time out on a Saturday and Sunday for your weekend break. Enjoy a little rest and relaxation on a Tuesday and Wednesday instead, or whichever two days best suit you. All that's important is that you have 48 hours to focus on yourself.

It's amazing how easy it is to swap a busy full-time job for another hectic schedule. Looking after beloved grandchildren, volunteering at the local school, attending an evening class—that much-yearned-for free time can quickly be consumed helping others, learning different skills, or mooching around the house. And while every minute may be relished, you can only be that fun-to-hang-out-with grandparent; the coffee-making, compassionate carer; or the eager-to-learn, diligent student if you dedicate a period of time every week to recharging your body and mind. You need the opportunity to relax, otherwise you'll risk burning yourself out.

Try to be strict with your boundaries (it can be tempting to be on call). To benefit fully, you need your two-day break to be a rejuvenating experience. Venture on a long walk without a phone; sit, listening to the radio in the yard without feeling the need to remove the weeds; unplug yourself from technology and don't answer emails. This is a time to slow down. Don't pay bills, run errands, or put on a quick laundry wash, you have other days of the week where this can happen. These two days are all about leisure and pleasure—enjoy.

WHY IT MATTERS. . .

. . .to make time for two consecutive free days

1 It's your reward

The pressures of everyday life can take their toll, even when you fill your waking hours surrounded by people you care about. There's no doubt it's a privilege to have enough spare time to spend with a young grandchild, a bereaved parent, or lonely neighbor. When you dedicate much of your life to others, and they rely on you, it's especially important to watch your own health and well-being. Allow yourself the reward of a couple of days off to escape from it all and take part in activities that bring you joy. Everyone deserves a break, you included.

2 Life needs structure

Days can easily and quickly start to blur into one another when no defined boundaries are set, and as a result you never truly get the chance to put your feet up and take it easy. Setting aside two clear days every week for your weekend gives life structure and reminds you to disconnect from the day-to-day. Forget about the routine for a while, do something different, or stop and sit down. Read a book, catch up on a few phone calls, or watch a new or favorite movie. Me-time is a time to relish.

3 Focus on fun

"All work and no play makes Jack a dull boy," as the saying goes, so even if you no longer work in a nine-to-five job, focus on fun on your two days off. People with a full-time job often claim they feel happier on a Saturday and Sunday, so ensure there is a 48-hour period—at least—when a big smile never leaves your face. Still not explored the countryside on your doorstep? Haven't yet started to play the violin you were given? Participate in activities that help to lift your mood. Share it with loved ones who make you laugh. This is what weekends are all about.

4 Rest requires downtime

While a weekend may not involve a morning lazing in bed, there is something to be said for having a couple of days when you don't need to be up at the crack of dawn to fit in a busy timetable. Give yourself a chance to recuperate. The only thing in your schedule should be rest. You can leisurely sip your coffee without watching the kitchen clock and flick through the pages of a favorite magazine knowing that the day ahead is yours to savor. What a wonderful thought.

5 Productivity improves

Weekends allow your head to clear. Just like when you go outside after concentrating for hours at your PC and that welcoming blast of fresh air wipes away the cobwebs, a change of scene and pace can make you feel more productive, spark creativity, and inspire you to achieve great things. Of course, it's easy to procrastinate if you feel you have a lot of spare time on your hands, which might mean your midweek weekend is truncated. Try to avoid this by setting a deadline ahead of your two-day rest. This will encourage you to step up a gear and get things done and out of the way, leaving your weekend days free.

6 Couples can reconnect

You may live with a spouse or partner, but how often do you spend relaxing time together? Devote weekends to being together, sharing experiences and making memories. Put some dates in your diary: Plan a couple of days at the coast (midweek breaks are often cheaper), arrange an evening at the theater, make a reservation at the new bistro in town—if you're able to spend more time in each other's company, take advantage of it. Turn the page for more ways to make the most of midweek treats.

MAKE TUESDAY THE NEW SATURDAY AND. . .

Avoid the crowds
Art galleries, tourist attractions, stores, beauty spots around the country—they're all much quieter during the week than they are at weekends. No one wants to spend precious time standing in a long line, vying for a inch of viewing space in an overcrowded exhibition hall or waiting for tourists to disperse so they can take a photograph—so don't. If you're planning a trip to a museum or other attraction, go online first to check out the quietest visiting times.

Grab a ticket
Weekend tickets for concerts, the opera, theater shows, and sporting events can be like gold dust. If you're able to attend an event on a Tuesday, or other weekday, the odds of securing a coveted seat are better. And catching a concert or other performance during the week will be much more appealing if, after a late night at the opera, you know you could stay over in town or have a lie-in the following morning.

Save on flights
According to Skyscanner, the travel fare aggregator website, if you wait until a Monday to book a flight, you can expect to pay around five percent less than the price you see online on a Saturday. Choose a Tuesday for your departure day, and as midweek flights tend to be less popular, travelers are often rewarded with cheaper fares. Saturday-afternoon flights can also be good value for money—weekend breakers typically want to leave on a Friday night or early Saturday morning.

Enjoy great deals
It's another simple case of supply and demand. During the week, and especially outside the summer vacation period, hotels and restaurants are not as busy as they are at weekends, so they try to entice people with special offers. Good-value deals can be found at Hotels.com—sign up online for free.

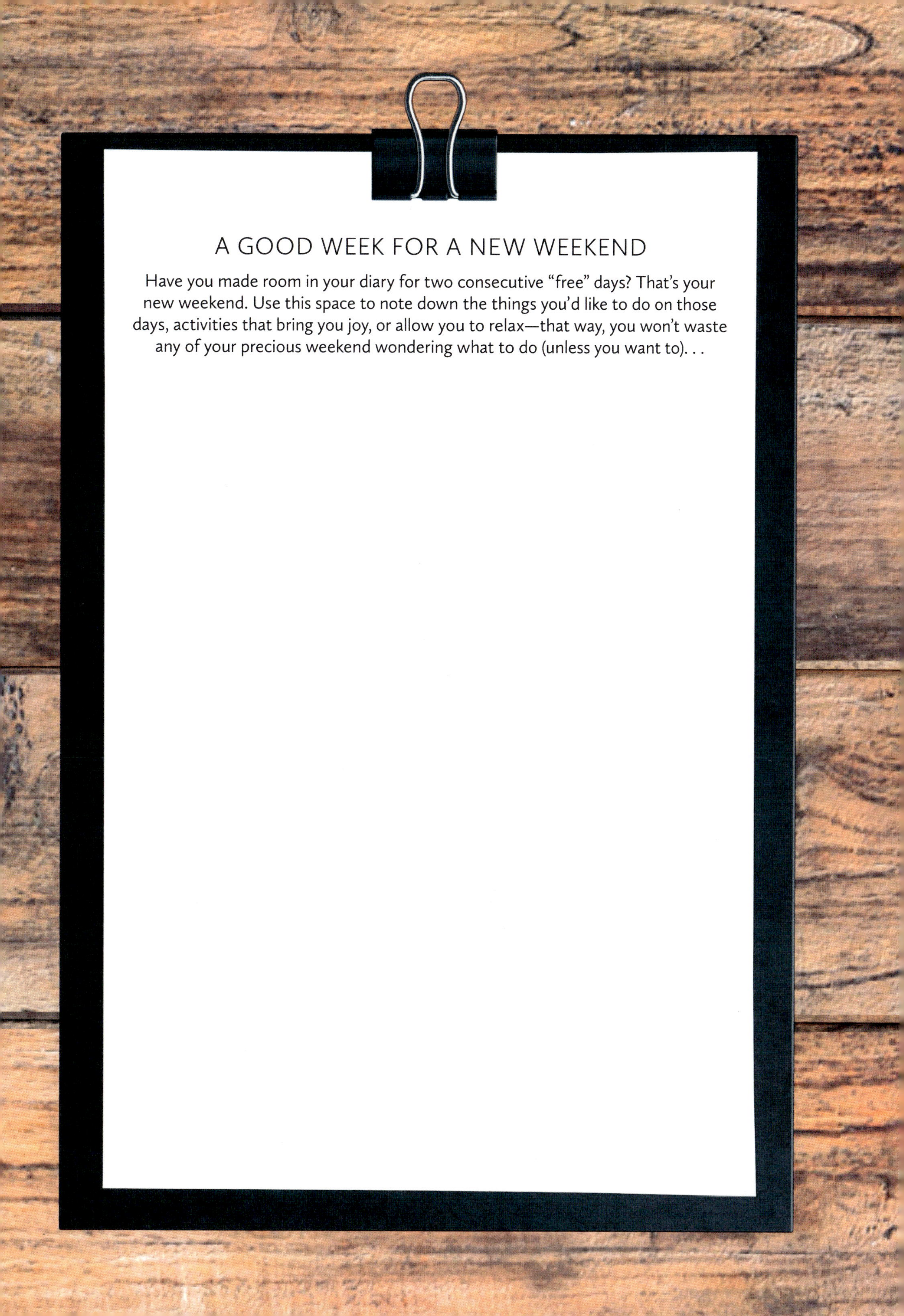

A GOOD WEEK FOR A NEW WEEKEND

Have you made room in your diary for two consecutive "free" days? That's your new weekend. Use this space to note down the things you'd like to do on those days, activities that bring you joy, or allow you to relax—that way, you won't waste any of your precious weekend wondering what to do (unless you want to). . .

The great outdoors

Why communing with nature has been given the green light

Woody Allen is one of the world's most celebrated wits, but the actor and movie director was surely wide of the mark when he once deadpanned: "I love nature, I just don't want to get any of it on me." For a more realistic view of the benefits of the great outdoors, it's perhaps better to study the observations of a man born almost 150 years earlier, Danish author Hans Christian Andersen. "Just living is not enough... one must have sunshine, freedom, and a little flower," he opined.

What is it about breathing in lungfuls of fresh air that causes many people to wax lyrical? The answer is simple: It enhances well-being in myriad ways. It's well known that enjoying the great wide outdoors can increase fitness. But various scientific studies, including a report last year by the UK's University of East Anglia (UEA), have officially confirmed that exposure to green spaces can also have long-term medical benefits. These health boosts include cutting the risk of heart disease, type 2 diabetes, and high blood pressure. Mentally, feelings of anxiety are reduced, while sleep duration increases.

"Spending time in nature certainly makes us feel healthier, but until now the impact on our long-term well-being hasn't been fully understood," says Caoimhe Twohig-Bennett from the UEA's Norwich Medical School. "We gathered evidence from over 140 studies involving more than 290 million people to see whether nature really does provide a health boost."

The research team looked at data from 20 countries, including the US, the UK, Spain, France, Germany, Australia, and Japan. It analyzed how the health of people with little access to green spaces compared to that of those with the highest amounts of exposure. Green space was defined as open, undeveloped land with natural vegetation, as well as urban parks, lawns, and trees.

"We found that spending time in, or living close to, natural green spaces is associated with diverse and significant health benefits. It reduces the risk of premature death from cardiovascular disease and type 2 diabetes," says Caoimhe. "People living closer to nature also had reduced diastolic blood pressure, heart rate, and stress. In fact, one of the really interesting things we discovered is that exposure to green spaces significantly reduces people's levels of salivary cortisol—a physiological marker of stress."

In Japan, many people swear by shinrin-yoku, or forest bathing, to improve the way they feel. Developed during the 1980s, it has become a cornerstone of preventive health care and healing in Far Eastern medicine. Scientists have established a robust body of evidence on the benefits of spending time under a canopy of trees. Now their research is helping to establish the practice throughout the world.

"Participants spend time in a forest, sitting, lying down, or walking around," says Caoimhe. "Our study shows that perhaps they have the right idea. Research suggests that phytoncides released by trees—organic compounds with antibacterial properties—could explain the health-boosting properties."

Study coauthor Professor Andy Jones adds: "We often reach for medication when we're unwell, but exposure to health-promoting environments is increasingly recognized as both preventing and helping treat disease. Our study shows that the size of these benefits can be enough to have a meaningful clinical impact."

The research team hopes its findings will prompt doctors and other healthcare professionals to recommend patients spend more time in natural areas. Caoimhe says: "We hope that this research will inspire people to get outside more and feel the health benefits for themselves. Hopefully our results will encourage policy makers and town planners to invest in the creation, regeneration, and maintenance of parks and green spaces, particularly in urban residential areas and deprived communities that could benefit the most."

Whether or not you're fortunate enough to live in an area where that is already happening, there are plenty of ways you can turn the environment to your advantage. It's suggested that just sitting outside for 20 minutes can give you as much energy as a cup of coffee, so why not ditch the caffeine?

WORDS: KIM SMITH. ILLUSTRATION: SARA THIELKER

Verdant vistas have been shown to make it feel easier to exercise, too. One study had cyclists pedaling in front of green, gray, and red video footage. Those who opted for green reported feeling less tired and more positive, leading to the conclusion that grass, trees, and plants give a psychological energy boost.

If you're not keen on pedal power, try joining a walking or bird-watching group for an alfresco fix. Gardening is, of course, another alternative, although it tends to be a pastime carried out in isolation. In the US there are community gardens, where it's possible to meet like-minded people. Gardening programs across the States give people the opportunity to plant and cultivate flowers, plants, and vegetables and help their town or neighborhood at the same time. The American Community Gardening Association has a wealth of resources aimed at supporting community gardens in your area, visit communitygarden.org for more information.

There are other health-enhancing properties of green space to consider, too. Sunlight is said to be better for your vision than artifical light and can help to mitigate pain. Breathing in airborne chemicals produced by greenery also increases white blood cells, which help to fight infections.

There's no need to pay for expensive aromatherapy as taking time to stop and smell roses, pine trees, and mown grass will provide instant serenity. If you're one of those people who is glued to a laptop or cell phone, switch it off—or lock it away—and spend a few days in the countryside gadget free. The electronic detox is guaranteed to make you relax and psychologists claim it will make you more creative.

In the depths of winter, with shorter days and less light, seasonal affective disorder can become a problem as well, causing symptoms such as anxiety and exhaustion. Doctors say this can be lessened by getting outdoors, provided you are sensible and wrap up against the chill.

Exposure to sunlight increases vitamin D, essential for health. It helps the body to absorb calcium, cutting the risk of osteoporosis and inflammation—a trigger for many chronic diseases. Just 15 minutes in the fresh air each day will help your body to receive the recommended dose and will speed up your recovery from illness or injury.

Being surrounded by nature restores mental focus, too, allowing you to ward off depression and stress, and prioritize the important things in life such as relationships and community involvement. The worldwide cost for treating mental health conditions is estimated by some to be an incredible $2trillion per year. Green spaces could reduce this bill as they are an organic way to buffer life's worries. This incorporates even those who move house to a greener neighborhood, something many choose to do in the process of downsizing. A study has proved they enjoy significantly better mental health in the first three post-relocation years.

So, what are you waiting for? Communing with nature, no matter how you choose to do it, is a positive, life-affirming way of boosting your energy, creativity, mental, and physical health. Give it the green light today.

In good company

Why people of all ages—and from all walks of life—can benefit from getting together and swapping stories

In the course of your working life you don't always have a lot of choice about the company you keep during the day. When you leave full-time employment, it's natural that you'll probably have less social interaction if you're not in an office full of people or regularly making the journey to and from work. Maybe you'll welcome that. Perhaps you didn't really enjoy Jeff's detailed descriptions of his wargames weekends that much anyway. On the other hand, you may feel anxious about the possibility of feeling increasingly isolated without the social structure that was part of your working week.

While you may feel that you'll have a number of relationships with people of a similar age because it's likely they've also left work, there's no reason why friendship should have an age limit. Many people are familiar with grim-sounding findings that have estimated the impact of loneliness on health can be akin to smoking 15 cigarettes a day. But it also seems that ensuring some variety in the company you keep is beneficial, too. Research by the AARP suggests that intergenerational interaction could boost your health. This could include your own children and grandchildren, of course, as well as any younger people that you know. In other words, it seems a pretty good idea to surround yourself with people of all ages.

Keep it fresh

The fact is, for even the most sociable of people, it can still take effort to forge new relationships. But the rewards are worthwhile and long-lasting. In retirement, taking up new activities and generally keeping yourself busy give your life some much-needed structure, and that also includes meeting new people, interacting with others in positive and productive ways, and developing friendships of different ages. The more groups, classes, and voluntary organizations you sign up for, the more likely it is that you'll meet a diverse group of people.

And while it's comforting to have friends that you've known for years, you may find that you tend to talk about the same subjects with them. If they're friends you've had for most of your life, you probably enjoy reminiscing about the past. There's nothing wrong with that, a little nostalgia is often wonderful, but don't limit yourself to it as you're giving yourself a narrow scope and missing out on a great deal.

Confirmation of that, if needed, comes from the very top. In the summer of 2018, following the wedding of Prince Harry and Meghan Markle, the newspapers were full of the special relationship that appeared to have blossomed between Queen Elizabeth, who is 92, and Meghan, 37, with photographs showing them very much at ease in each other's company. It has been suggested that the Queen forged this relationship with the Duchess of Sussex precisely because she wants the royal family to be—and to be seen to be—open to change.

A wider perspective

Elizabeth Knight, 73, finds that a combination of activities, including various keep-fit classes, volunteering, and church groups, brings her into contact with all sorts of people. "A lot of those are people younger than me," she says of the volunteer groups. "Most of my friends are younger, I don't know why, it just happens to be that way. And there are loads of classes you can go to and meet the most lovely people. But I think you have to make an effort. If there's someone you really get on with, you just have to say: 'Why don't you stop by for coffee?' It's not enough simply to say: 'Well that was great, take care, bye.' You do have to work on it.

"And if you've got an interested, active mind, a younger person will find you interesting. I think this idea of: 'Oh, I'm 70, I'm not very interesting any more, what am I going to talk to people about?' is not the right way to approach life. I see it as really important to have young people as friends and, to be honest, I don't want to be surrounded by golden oldies—so I'm not. And my children are in their late 30s and early 40s now, and of course their friends are young. So I've got many more young friends than older ones."

Elizabeth says that she doesn't think she talks to younger people differently than older ones. "I just take people as they are. I'm not one of those people who says: 'Oh well, it was much better in my day.' I tend to believe that old people today think that the past was golden and that every day the sun shone. But it wasn't like that at all. It was tough and there were strikes and food shortages. Perhaps I'm a bit more gentle with young people because I think things like the internet and social media make life very hard for them—the idea that they've all got to keep up with everybody else."

Generation gap

Partly because of the different kinds of pressures on young people today, Elizabeth has found it interesting to read a number of books on how to bring up teenagers. "I wanted to know how teenagers operate today. I think older people should read up on why teenagers and young people behave as they do. There are huge pressures on them that we never had when we were young. It's been quite an eye-opener—we now understand why teenagers are the way they are, we

"Do stuff. Be clenched, curious... Pay attention... Attention is vitality. It connects you with others. It makes you eager. Stay eager"

SUSAN SONTAG

understand why they need so much more sleep. It was really interesting. I ended up being able to see why young people are so often misunderstood."

Reaching out

Someone else who finds that her interests lead her to meet an incredibly diverse group of people is Deborah Collins, 61, who has a number of groups, projects, and volunteer work filling her time since leaving work in 2017. She also continues to attend a long-standing writers' group, which includes age-diverse members from twenty-somethings to octogenarians. Deborah is particularly keen to be able to devote more time to writing poetry and collating existing poems, which she intends to publish independently. That might seem to be a fairly solitary pursuit, but she has recently started attending poetry evenings to perform her poems at a monthly local event and a more popular one downtown.

"There's a big mixture of age groups, from people who are about 20 years old to those in their 70s, maybe older than that. And different cultural backgrounds, different races and religions. Someone had warned me that I might find it intimidating performing in front of an audience of other poets, so I thought I'd go along as a member of the audience first.

"And as the night went on, I thought: 'This is great, the audience is not critiquing people, they're just giving them lots of applause and cheers.' It was rather lovely, actually. So a week or two later I went along and performed myself and they were very warm and supportive, and cheered and clapped at the end."

So don't subscribe to those clichés of older people being set in their ways and having nothing in common with younger ones. If you've lived for six decades or more, it pays to remember that you've got a lifetime's worth of experience (and all the associated stories) behind you. It's probable that friends of any age will relate to a story of a mortifying incident, eye-opening encounter, or life-changing vacation—they just might express it slightly differently.

Inner peace

Practicing meditation for a few minutes every day can help relieve chronic health issues, aid relaxation, and boost mental clarity

Sit quietly, close your eyes, gaze inward. . . Have you thought about meditating? Maybe you have, but were too busy to give it time, or you didn't know where to start. Or maybe you felt you couldn't sit still for any length of time, especially cross-legged and when suffering from a chattering, restless mind.

The good news is interest in meditation has grown in recent years and so has the availability of help and tuition if you're new to it. Better still, much of this support is free and accessible online if you don't want to learn one-to-one or in a group. And you don't need to sit in a lotus position—a cozy armchair is every bit as good.

Meditation has been around for more than 3,000 years—and there are countless studies and anecdotal reports on its benefits and why establishing a meditation practice is well worth the effort. It can help to improve digestion, blood pressure, and chronic pain and fatigue; aid relaxation, and sleep, smoking, drinking and weight management; and boost your creative flow, mental clarity, and even spiritual growth.

Celebrity following

Its high-profile advocates include Oprah Winfrey, who says: "I am 100 percent better when I do it," Paul McCartney, who insists: "In moments of madness, meditation has helped me find moments of serenity," and Clint Eastwood and Nicole Kidman, who practice transcendental meditation (TM). Movie director David Lynch is so passionate about the latter method that he set up schools teaching TM across the US.

Andy Puddicombe is a meditation and mindfulness expert (and former monk) whose brainchild is Headspace. Its website is a wealth of information and exercises on the subject and has this message: "Meditation isn't about becoming a different person, a new person, or even a better person. It's about training in awareness and getting a healthy sense of perspective. You're not trying to turn off your thoughts or feelings. You're learning to observe them without judgment. Eventually, you may start to better understand them as well."

Simplicity

Meditation can be tailored according to your needs, being a pleasant, calming refresher when your energies are flagging, or a profound personal journey deep into the inner recesses of your heart and mind. It can help you to tap into what you really want and get a clearer picture of yourself, your goals, and place in your world. And it can be started at any age, says Will Williams, a top meditation teacher. "It is a tool for humans regardless of age, background, or experience—there is no difference to how you learn, and how I teach. What is key across the board is its simplicity."

Will turned to meditation 10 years ago, having experienced long bouts of stress and stress-related insomnia. He was drawn to vedic meditation, which he describes as: "One of the most ancient and easiest to learn techniques." For Will, turning to meditation brought huge personal benefits (and better sleeping patterns), and he started teaching meditation. He now teaches in London, England, and at retreats.

"I've taught all ages. I had a remarkable couple from Switzerland who were 85 and 86; they said meditation gave them a new lease of life," says Will. "It was inspiring

"In moments of madness, meditation has helped me find moments of serenity"

PAUL McCARTNEY

---

to see how it improved their energy and zest. They hadn't changed a thing apart from learning how to meditate."

He adds: "Regular practice helps root you in the now so you can appreciate the joys of today, regardless of what might happen tomorrow. It can free you of fears, which with self-esteem issues, can hold you back. It can alleviate grief for lost loved ones, and regrets about things you did or didn't do in life. Of course, it doesn't make all problems go away but it can help you tackle them so the real you can begin to shine again.'

Inner calm

One great change meditators report is a feeling of inner calm: "Many find they are more at peace with themselves and everything; they're more comfortable in their own skin." And, of course, people are drawn to practice meditation in the first place for a range of different reasons: "Some want to connect to their own humanity. Others have felt lonely since giving up work or their family have left home. Meditation can help them reconnect to the person they were before they had the label of mother or father or this or that job title."

James, 75, had a long career as a psychologist. "I tried to retire a few years ago, but when I cut my working hours, I began to suffer from anxiety, depression—a feeling of no purpose, thinking: 'What's it all about?'" He says he felt anxiety about death: "All those things one thinks about in one's 70s." He didn't want to take medication, but when a friend suggested he try meditation, he went for it. "I'd always liked the idea of it and that it has been around for centuries—I was just too busy to try it before."

It wasn't an immediate success, he admits: "Nothing much happened at first. It took a while to soak in. I had to work at it." When he went on a four-day retreat, where he was meditating for 20 minutes twice a day and doing yoga too, he felt he really clicked with it. "I found it helped me to stop thinking and start living—to be more in my body and not so much in my head. It put my anxiety and depression into perspective. I am more content. I wouldn't say happy, as I see that as a state, but I've been able to think about more difficult areas in my life."

He says one of the biggest changes meditation has made for him is he's stopped drinking alcohol. "I loved wine, especially as I have a house in France and spend a lot of my time there. I wasn't even close to being an alcoholic, but I couldn't stop at one glass. Drinking had become a habit, not a pleasure. Once I started meditating, I began thinking about the social conditioning around alcohol, and I thought 'no,' and I stopped. It was easy. It's been great for me. I don't want to run my life by it, I want to use it for me."

Mindfulness

Mindfulness is a form of meditation that has over the years gained popularity and reach and is suggested as a way to pay attention to the present moment and improve mental well-being. Mindfulness is the ability to be present, to rest in the here and now, and be fully engaged with whatever you're doing in the moment.

A study by the University of California looked at whether mindfulness meditation could reduce feelings of loneliness. Adults (mostly women) aged 55 to 85, took an eight-week course of mindfulness-based stress reduction (MBSR), which involved 30 minutes' meditation at home per day plus weekly group meetings and a one-day retreat, as well as breathing techniques and other body awareness skills. Those who meditated reported less loneliness—and their blood tests showed a significant drop in the expression of inflammation-related genes (chronic inflammation being a marker of physical and psychological disorder).

Sherri Saxe took up mindfulness meditation to calm anxieties around family issues. She followed a five-senses meditation where you notice what you're hearing, smelling, tasting, seeing, and feeling on your body, for a period of 10 to 40 minutes. "If my mind wanders, I gently bring it back like a little puppy," she writes on her website Sixty+Me. "For each sense, the trick is to really deeply focus on it and tune into the smallest details... It keeps my mind occupied and focused on slow, restful, present-moment things." After meditating she feels "relaxed, with a delicious sense of well-being... If I get an upsetting text or phone call, I am much less ruffled by it."

While there is no evidence to suggest meditation can prevent, treat, or cure serious disease, the American Cancer Society recommends it as a useful complementary therapy. Studies show mindfulness-based stress reduction can help to relax, relieve some symptoms and improve quality of life; that it can improve concentration and mood, and reduce depression and anxiety. But it can take time to feel these benefits.

READY TO START MEDITATING?

According to Headspace: *"There's no such thing as perfect meditation. Sometimes your focus will wander or you'll forget to follow your breath. That's okay. It's part of the experience. What's most important is to meditate consistently. It's one of those things where the journey is more important than the destination." You might want to take some time now to consider which type of meditation (see below) works best for you...*

Guided meditation is where you are led through the experience. You can either do this by attending a class, or listening to a meditation on a CD or any verbal instruction (such as on YouTube). Guided meditation can relate to physical and mental well-being, or to a topic such as manifesting dreams and wishes. It can be particularly useful for beginners who need extra guidance or those with active minds who need help focusing.

Loving-kindness meditation uses words, images, and feelings to invoke qualities of love and friendliness toward yourself and others. Said to help change your perception of the world in a positive way. Like other forms of meditation, it can help with your relationships and connections with others, physical healing, and mental well-being.

Mindfulness meditation encompasses everyday practices including eating, walking, looking at the world, sitting in stillness. According to the Buddhist monk and teacher Thich Nhat Hanh: "Mindfulness helps you to go home to the present." Said by many to be life-changing, its roots are steeped in the Buddhist tradition, and it helps you to accept all that arises without judgment and be in the moment. Good for attention, decreasing stress, gaining a positive mood, and self-awareness.

Mantra meditation is a feature of transcendental and vedic meditation, and other practices. A mantra can be a sound—or sounds, words, or phrases—which is repeated (often silently) during a session, to keep the mind focused and help the meditator reach a higher state of consciousness. Says Will, who's planning to launch a new guided meditation app: "We use repetition of the mantra, which is one of the most subtle sensory experiences but goes deeper, for a powerful healing outcome." Many mantras are sounds with no meaning (so you're not distracted). A good practice for those who like structure and need clarity around their goals.

Breathing meditation can bring your focus back into the present moment and help you take more conscious decisions. It plays on the mind-body connection—as the mind calms, so does the body and vice-versa. Or as psychologist James says: "You cannot separate body from mind, you can't be physically hurt without being mentally hurt, and vice-versa." Breathing meditation can help you understand and appreciate how you can influence your own physical and mental well-being. It helps reduce stress immediately, helps to ground you, clears and centers the mind and revitalizes and improves physical well-being. Find breathing meditation workshops through yoga and wellness studios and online.

For more information, visit willwilliamsmeditation.co.uk

TRY THIS SIMPLE EXERCISE. . .

You can choose to focus on your breath or on a mantra. If you opt for a mantra, go for a word or short phrase that has no specific meaning for you, such as "so hum."

1. Sit comfortably—this can be in a chair or sitting up in bed. You can lie down but if you're tired you may fall asleep. The idea of meditation is to achieve a state of relaxed alertness.
2. Close your eyes. Make no effort to control the breath, simply breathe naturally.
3. Focus your attention on the breath, observing how it enters the nostrils with cool air and exits the nostrils with warmed air. If you choose to work with a mantra, allow it to enter your mind, and let it repeat gently without forcing it.
4. If your mind wanders, gently return your focus back to your breath or to the mantra.

Begin with meditating for between five and 10 minutes, practicing for longer periods when you feel more comfortable with it.

Pet power

Do you want to stay healthy in both body and mind? Sharing your home with a cat, dog, or even a rabbit may be the answer

Keen to keep your blood pressure down? Reduce your stress levels? Improve your mood? If the answer is yes, then perhaps now is the time to consider getting a pet. Whether it's a dog providing unconditional love, a cat purring on your lap, or a hamster raising a smile with its comical cheeks, daily contact with a pet can have physiological and psychological benefits.

Stroking a dog, cat, or other furry friend for just 15 minutes is believed to lower blood pressure. The simple action releases a chemical in the body called oxytocin, sometimes known as the "cuddle hormone," which has a calming and soothing effect. It's no wonder then that 95 percent of pet owners in the US think of their pet as a member of the family.

All types of pets can have an impact. A brisk 30-minute walk every day with a faithful pal can, according to the Stroke Association, help to prevent and control high blood pressure, and reduce the risk of a stroke. New dog owners often observe an improvement in their fitness, and they develop stronger muscles and bones as a result of regular low-impact exercise.

Cats have their role to play too. A Cats Protection survey reveals that the majority of people who own a cat feel it has a positive impact on their well-being, with over three-quarters of them claiming it improves their mental health—having a cat means they are able to cope better with everyday life.

Psychologists at Miami University and Saint Louis University agree. They recently conducted three experiments on the benefits of pet ownership, the results of which were subsequently published by the American Psychological Association. The studies showed that pet owners had improved well-being in various areas, including better self-esteem and improved fitness. Pets were also seen to alleviate loneliness, provide a sense of purpose, and make owners more extroverted and less fearful. Indeed, companionship is the reason many people decide to get a pet, especially in later life when family may have left home or you find yourself on your own.

Man's (and woman's) best friend

Anyone new to an area or on the lookout for a new circle of acquaintances will have no trouble with introductions among the dog-walking community if they've a hound in tow. Turn up at a regular time to a park or stretch of beach and the same faces will be around day in, day out. With a dog by your side, not only will you feel safer, you've got the perfect ice breaker.

Before getting a dog, however, you'll need to decide which breed best suits your lifestyle. Some, such as the Siberian husky, demand daily grooming. Border collies need constant stimulation. Bulldogs can suffer from separation anxiety. But they all give you heaps of unconditional love in return for your care and affection. As for a Labrador Retriever, he may have an easygoing personality but don't mistake that for low energy. Labs ideally need at least an hour of exercise a day—a perfect companion if you love being outdoors.

If you're still unsure if dog ownership is for you, have a trial run. Offer to look after a friend or neighbor's dog. Alternatively, sign up to an app like Bark'N'Borrow, which connects dog owners with trusted dog sitters and walker. Animal shelters rely on fosterers to provide temporary homes for animals in their care. That's a good option if you're able to look after an animal for a few months or so, but not able to commit long-term.

"Animals are such agreeable friends—they ask no questions, they pass no criticisms"

GEORGE ELIOT

Commitment and costs

On the subject of commitment, this doesn't just involve braving a blustery morning to take your pooch for a walk (which can actually be quite invigorating). You'll also need to factor in costs. On average, depending on the size of your dog, they will vary between $2 and $5 a day—not excessive when you take into account this covers food, bedding, pet insurance, grooming costs, regular flea and worm treatments, poop bags, and annual vaccinations.

Caring for a cat—the second most popular pet in the US—costs, on average, just over $2.50 a day. Generally, cats are easier to look after. Unlike dogs, you can leave them for long periods of time during the day and they'll barely notice you're not there. Remember, though, that although you feed your tom cat, there's no guarantee that he'll snuggle up on your lap in the night. He may prefer the company of the neighbors. As the saying goes, dogs have masters, cats have servants.

Future planning

Pets quickly become part of the family, and as such you'll want to make sure they're well looked after when you're on vacation, or if something unexpected happens, like a hospital stay. As the average dog lives between 10 and 13 years, there's also the worry that your pet may survive you—what happens then?

If you're sick for a few days, away for a weekend, or taking a longer vacation, hopefully neighbors, family, or friends will rally round and offer to look after Fido or Felix. If not, there are options. Dog walkers and cat sitters can help. Ask locally for recommendations. In the event of a crisis, a local animal welfare charity could offer help via their network of volunteers.

For peace of mind, it may be worth adding a provision to your will to make sure that your beloved pet will be well cared for in the future.

The dog debate

Are healthy people more likely to get a dog, or does owning a dog make you healthier? This was much debated last year after the release of a survey from a team at Uppsala University in Sweden, who looked at data from more than 3.4 million people aged between 40 and 80 in order to evaluate the association between dog ownership and long-term cardiovascular health.

The main findings suggested that having a dog was associated with a 23 percent reduction in death from heart disease. For those living alone, there was further good news. Compared to single nonpet owners, the results showed that single dog owners reduced their risk of death by a third, with an 11 percent reduction in the risk of a heart attack.

Dr. Mike Knapton, associate medical director at the British Heart Foundation in the UK, commented: "Owning a dog is associated with reduced mortality and risk of having heart disease. We cannot infer a causal relationship, however dog ownership is associated with increased physical activity, improved psycho-social well-being, and socialization, all of which are associated with reduced cardiovascular disease mortality. So, it is plausible the effect is mediated through these mechanisms. Alternatively, it could be reverse causality—people who are fitter and more active are more likely to own a dog.

"Dog ownership has many benefits, and we may now be able to count better heart health as one of them. However, as many may agree, the main reason for owning a dog is the sheer joy." The bonds between humans and animals are powerful, and the positive correlation between pets and happiness is undeniable.

Loss after loss

Coping with repeated losses in your life—be they bereavements, friends moving away, or the distancing of once-close colleagues—can be hard, but it is possible to move forward again

You may well know the expression: "Life is what happens while you're busy making other plans," and throughout your own life have come to understand that unexpected events are par for the course. At particular times, however, certain events may become more frequent and predictably consistent, such as experiencing repeated losses as you get older.

Perhaps you've experienced the death of a close friend, the distancing of formerly close colleagues as you come out of a working environment, or the death of a much-beloved pet. And that's before you start thinking about other less tangible losses that can be experienced, such as physical health, self-identity, or status.

What effect do repeated losses have on an individual? How do you cope with and prepare for a stage of life that throws up these experiences more commonly? Are there ways to live alongside them so that you can continue to thrive, to grow, and start to move forward again?

What counts as loss?

While this question might seem straightforward, sometimes it can be difficult to define what counts as a loss. It can be internal and closely tied to how you view yourself, such as a perceived loss of status or self-identity, or external, such as the deaths of friends or loved ones. It can also be defined as: "The feeling of grief after losing someone or something of value." In other words, loss is about personal experience and perception, as opposed to the views of others on what does or doesn't count as a loss.

While loss often means bereavement, this isn't always the case. It may relate to friends who have decided to move away, or relationships with significant people that have suddenly changed because of ill health, for example. Losses may also be those that you anticipate. Julie* says that she struggles with the thought of future losses: "I worry about how I will cope with the loss of people very close to me. I believe you feel more vulnerable and anxious as the years go by. . . it makes you think of your own vulnerability and how you will cope in the future with failing health and independence."

Making sense of your experiences

Has it felt like each loss hits you harder than the one before it? Loss commonly functions on a "thread" basis, with each new loss experienced acting as a trigger to remind you of previous ones. Processing several can require a high level of energy and personal resources. In the case of multiple losses, perhaps in relatively quick succession over a year or two, you may be left with a numb feeling, like you've shut down and don't know who you are any more. While it can be scary, this is actually a survival mechanism designed to protect you from being overwhelmed and experiencing more than you can cope with. It is important to give yourself permission to feel affected or overwhelmed by what you have experienced. Time, care, and support is needed for you to be able to deal with each loss.

Letting yourself grieve

Grief is a process that is commonly described as consisting of a number of stages. In their model of grief, Elisabeth Kübler-Ross and David Kessler describe five stages: denial, anger, bargaining, depression, and acceptance. All these stages are part of the normal process of grieving, and won't necessarily be experienced in a linear way or with a set time limit and you may dip in and out of these emotions for some time. These same stages can also roughly equate to the process of adjustment you might go through for a loss that isn't typically associated with bereavement.

Joanna Beazley Richards, a clinical psychologist and psychotherapist, says that the impact of multiple losses on individuals varies greatly: "Some people use the experience to look again at their lives and to take stock of their priorities; to value their remaining friends and loved ones more; to appreciate that life is finite and that they need to experience every moment fully and deeply.

"The full, deep experiencing of grief has been shown to aid an increased sense of well-being and capacity for joy. Problems come when people do not surrender to grief and mourning, and somehow block it."

Self-care

Taking care of yourself while managing a number of losses is crucial. Help your body to be strong and well through eating regular meals and good nutrition. Make time to move about through the day, as the mind has a habit of getting stuck in difficult thoughts when the body is static. Take the time to focus on good sleep habits as much as possible, having a regular wind-down routine, bedtime, and wake time. Make the time and effort to see others when you are ready. This may mean finding a new person to meet for a weekly coffee, or joining a new group or community that you hadn't considered previously. Julie has found that taking one day at a time has helped: "Try not to worry about what has not yet happened and look at what positive things you have achieved each day."

Lack of validation

Culturally, you may come across notions about how loss and grief should be coped with at different stages of life, for example that losses in one's older years are less meaningful because they are to be expected. Joanna says: "The worst thing to do is just to get on with it. Unfortunately some people are expected to do that, and may even be praised when they do. This can really store up trouble for the person, and is related to the onset of physical problems."

Berating yourself for feeling a certain way about the losses you experience in your life, or trying to convince yourself that you should be feeling differently, is generally futile. Such approaches create resistance and additional struggle. To deny your losses, or convince yourself that they shouldn't affect you, is to do yourself, and your well-being, a great disservice.

Celebrating what was

It's worth reminding yourself that any pain you have from a loss is directly connected to the love and value that person or being brought into your life. And that is something to celebrate. When you feel ready, think about how you would best like to honor them. Perhaps you might like to collect your favorite pictures or anecdotes about them into a scrapbook, frame a meaningful picture of you both or write them a letter with all the things you would like to say to them now. If you have others who knew and valued them too, you might like to get together and share stories about them or talk about what made them so important to you. An additional uplifting technique is to imagine what the lost individual would have said to you in a particular situation.

Nurturing growth after multiple losses

Experiencing multiple losses can knock you sideways, but you can regain control and meaning in your life. When you can, and with courage, let life and loss flow around you, much like the water in a stream—therein lies a sense of freedom. Make a point of cherishing what you have to love and value in your life in the here and now, while keeping a place for those lost in your heart. As social reformer Havelock Ellis said: "All the art of living lies in a fine mingling of letting go and holding on."

Words: **Dr. Sarah Maynard**
Sarah is a clinical psychologist and mindfulness practitioner. For more information, visit wildandpreciousminds.com

COPING IF FRIENDS HAVE MOVED AWAY

- Use social media to stay connected, post pictures that will help to show what you're up to now, and comment on the things they share.
- If circumstances allow, plan a trip to meet up—put the details in your diary. Such plans can be wonderful and motivating to look forward to, keeping you going through the tougher days.
- Rediscover the art of letter writing. It can be a lovely surprise to receive a letter or a card in the mail—it lets a person know that someone out there is thinking about them, particularly if they live on their own or don't have regular company.
- Share your memories and send photos of things that are happening in your life now, perhaps with younger family members or somewhere you have visited recently.

Additional help can be beneficial at any age to cope with multiple losses and a first point of call should be your doctor or a trained counselor. Other helpful resources include:

Coping with loss and loneliness—*griefnet.org*
Further information on grief—*grief.com*

Take a closer look

It's easy to have one's head turned by a gallery's headline-grabbing exhibition. But waiting among its permanent collection, far from the stress and elbows of the crowd, are priceless gems. Give them 30 minutes of your time and these patient stalwarts will reward your spirit and mind

The world's galleries are filled with thousands of pieces of artwork ready and waiting to be viewed and assessed. The reality, however, is that each visitor may view an individual painting for just a few seconds before moving on to the next. They'll register only the initial appearance of the work and rarely have or take the time to get under its skin and understand its meanings or intentions. This seems a great shame, especially when the artist could have been working for months on preparatory sketches and planning before spending months and perhaps even years on the painting itself. Artwork deserves more time.

Each year, the larger galleries put together exciting temporary exhibitions by big-name, popular artists. It gains them media attention and (generally) guaranteed visitors who grab the chance to see a rare collection of work before the window of opportunity expires. The downside is the exhibitions often feel overcrowded and afford little opportunity to slow down and spend time absorbing each piece of artwork—the streams of people constantly usher you on to the next sculpture or painting, allowing only snapshots over other people's shoulders.

The regulars

But what about the ever-present paintings in the world's galleries—the stalwarts that are there every day, year in, year out, and are so often forgotten in the rush to see the big, coverage-generating event? They'll still be there once the season's spectacular is over and the crowds have died down. And they'll still be waiting patiently in the permanent collections for you to discover and explore them more deeply.

Instead of queuing with the stressed hordes to (not) see a collection of artwork, how about doing the opposite? Carefully select a single piece of artwork from a gallery's permanent collection, visit at a peaceful time of day, and study it intimately. Could your perceptions of this work change over a 30-minute time span? Perhaps you'll notice something that wasn't apparent at first. Maybe you'll appreciate its techniques and interpret its meaning more than if you'd viewed it for mere seconds before feeling pressured to move on.

There are enormous physical and mental health benefits brought about by visiting a gallery this way. The more mindful approach of sitting in a quiet space to absorb one painting for a significant length of time can be a far more relaxing and enlightening experience. Your body has the time to slow down while you immerse yourself within the artwork.

You can use your imagination to step inside the painting, living it, traveling around the scene to survey it in more detail. This allows you to engage more of your senses than just your sight. You can taste the succulent fruit on a table or smell the flowers blooming within the midsummer meadow. You can hear the heated debate of a group of people or shiver with cold as the storm rages within the seascape.

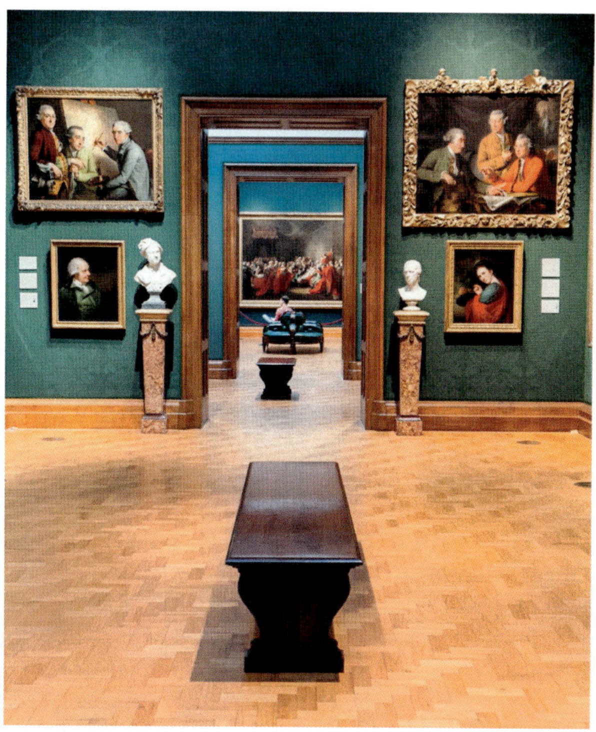

See art afresh

As you move around the gallery, respectfully watching people's reactions to particular artworks or listening to comments made about a painting can be surprisingly thought-provoking. Everybody will interpret artwork differently and approach it from different angles. It can be quite illuminating to hear other points of view that might open up some aspects of the artwork that you hadn't initially considered.

Classically trained artists throughout history, for instance, learned to understand the human proportions or light and shadow by sketching sculptures from Ancient Rome or Greece. While not everybody would be comfortable doing this, taking notes or producing sketches of elements of a painting that intrigue you can help you to understand more fully the themes or techniques employed by an artist.

If this appeals, try doing some research in advance of arriving at the gallery or museum. You don't want to get there only to find your favored piece, which hasn't been outside the gallery's walls for 50-plus years, is on loan to another country. Gallery websites provide up-to-date information about which pieces of work are currently on view and often feature helpful biographies or notes about an author's techniques. What you choose to view is, of course, down to location, timings, and, most importantly, personal taste, but spending 30 minutes in the company of a permanent-collection artwork that intrigues and fascinates will broaden the mind, nourish the soul, and keep you far from the madding crowds.

They may not be to everyone's taste, but here are a few paintings for which we'd happily set aside a peaceful half an hour to contemplate. We invite you to take a closer look...

Napoleon Crossing the Alps, by Jacques-Louis David (1801). Château de Malmaison, Paris

(*Pictured right*) In the ambitious portrait, Jacques Louis David glorifies the Emperor Napoleon by placing him upon a rearing horse, heroically leading his army toward the invasion of Northern Italy. Napoleon chose the scene himself, but reportedly did not sit for the artist. Instead, he lent him the outfit that can be seen in the painting. David's son sat on the top of a ladder to create the pose. Knowing this only makes the portrait more impressive. An interesting element of the work is the contrast between the calm face of Napoleon and the crazed expression of the fiery steed upon which he sits. Another would be the carved names of other leaders who led their armies through the Alps, which appear beneath the rearing horse.

Tiger in a Tropical Storm, by Henri Rousseau (1891). The National Gallery, London

This striking painting is impossible to walk past without stopping. For years, Henri Rousseau's work was ridiculed for its primitive style. This is because he was largely a self-taught artist. But it makes his work unique and personal and with this artwork you can travel into it and feel the elements. The tiger looks terrified and you can hear the thunder booming through the landscape. The wind forces the vegetation to lean at a diagonal slant, while in the background the lightning rips across the sky at the same angle. Rousseau even trailed thin strands of paint diagonally across the canvas to create a shimmering rain effect, which can only be seen when standing in front of the artwork. Rousseau, who never visited the jungle, created the dazzling variety of vegetation by visiting the local botanical gardens.

Wheatfield with Crows, by Vincent Van Gogh (1890). Rijkmuseum Vincent Van Gogh, Amsterdam

Considering Van Gogh had a special talent for creating landscapes with feeling, this is one of his final and most emotionally charged pieces. The painting fizzes with energy. At the top, the dark clouds swell and roll while sharp, angular crows stalk the scene, haunting the viewer. Beneath this, the wheat blazes like fire. The artwork feels claustrophobic to most observers. The tracks beneath the wheatfield lead to nowhere and there's no escape. Step closer to the work and you can see the thickness of the paint applied onto the canvas. You can feel Van Gogh's dark mood within the brushstrokes as he leaves something of himself within the paint. The artwork creates a window into the emotional state of Van Gogh as he neared the end of his tortured life. This landscape has a lot to say.

Christina's World, by Andrew Wyeth (1948). MOMA, New York

(*Pictured far right*) Among the striking powerhouse paintings found in New York's Museum of Modern Art, this one hangs on the wall in quiet, subtle brilliance. Christina, crippled by polio as a child, was a friend of Andrew Wyeth. Studying the figure within the scene, you catch a glimpse of her frailty through her skeletal arms. She gazes upon her seemingly unreachable home on the horizon. The field of grass has no depth, making it an unscaleable wall. In 1969, when Christina Olson died in the house depicted within the artwork, she had no idea that Wyeth's image of her had become one of the most recognizable paintings in all of American Art.

Self Portrait as Saint Catherine of Alexandria,
by Artemisia Gentileschi (1615-1617).
The National Gallery, London*

(*Pictured right*) This newly discovered and recently restored artwork, which was bought by the National in July 2018 for £3.6million ($4.5million), goes a little way to redressing the pitifully low number of artworks (currently 20) by female artists in its collection. It was created in a time when male artists dominated the art world and few women had the opportunity to succeed. This makes the painting even more significant. It depicts the artist as Saint Catherine of Alexandria, who was a strong female heroine, similar to how Artemisia Gentileschi is now seen herself. The subtle light and shadow creates soft edges on the face, which evokes images by masters such as Leonardo Da Vinci and Raphael. Artemisia's father, Orazio, was also an artist and, incredibly, has work exhibited in the same gallery.

Words: Colin Davies
Colin is an art teacher and practicing portrait artist

It's a date!

Looking for a new relationship, but don't know where to begin? Follow our tips to get back into the dating game

Finding love again is exciting whatever your age—enjoying those same feelings of a fluttering heart and the anticipation of a next meeting that you first experienced when in your teens. More and more people are finding love in later life and there are now many online dating sites aimed at the over-60s. But getting to the point where you've met someone special can take time and courage. There's a difference between thinking about dating and taking action, and if you haven't been on a date for some time, it can feel like a leap into the unknown.

Are you ready to date?

First, consider whether you are really ready to start dating again. If you have come to the end of a long-term relationship or are on your own because of a bereavement, it can be difficult to gauge whether you're ready to meet someone new.

Perhaps this is the first time you've been on your own. It may be that friends and family have taken to pressurizing you into dating. It can take time before you are ready. If you're struggling to get over a past love, it's hard to commit again. Spend time living on your own for a while, as you adjust to this new phase in your life and get to know yourself as a single person, rather than as half of a couple. That way, when you do start dating, you'll have more of a sense of who you are and what you really want from a new relationship.

Manage expectations

Whatever your age, it's only natural to get caught up in the excitement of it all when you start dating, but managing your expectations means you make healthy connections and feel good about yourself throughout the process.

Try to keep an open mind when you meet someone new. It's easy to start nit-picking or comparing your date to a past love, but think about the overall feeling you have being in the other person's company. If you generally feel comfortable with them and have shared interests, it's worth going on a second date to see where it will lead. If you have a long checklist of attributes that you're looking for, you may be waiting a long time. He or she may not look like George Clooney or Helen Mirren, but be the kindest of people—a quality that can go a long way in life.

Keep conversation light

You're not alone if you feel nervous on your first date. They'll probably be feeling the same way. Try to keep the conversation light, avoid giving your whole life history, and remember that if they start talking endlessly about something you find dull, this may just be nerves. As you get to know each other and relax, you'll be able to see how well the conversation flows.

After the first date

You've met someone you like, but what now? Don't feel flat if you don't hear back from them immediately—they may not be someone who expects constant communication, or they may be busy and don't know you are waiting for a sign that they're keen on you. Until you're properly committed to each other, keep an open mind and see a number of people at the same time. Be open about the fact you're seeing other people, if asked. Honesty is always the best policy when dating. As your feelings for someone develop you can have that conversation about seeing each other exclusively.

Enjoy the experience

Now is a great time to start dating. The rise in online dating sites has taken the stigma away from meeting someone new. Now people are living (and keeping fitter) for longer, they're more open to the idea that they're entitled to a happy relationship whatever their age. Remember always to be yourself when you meet someone new. Let them see the real you—and enjoy the journey.

WHERE TO MEET?

When you are on your own, it can be hard to imagine how you'll actually meet someone new, but there are plenty of opportunities to get back into the dating game

1 **Start a new activity**
Take a class in something you've never tried before—pottery, poker, a foreign language. You'll expand your knowledge while potentially meeting new people, particularly if you look for a class that's near to you, but not on your doorstep. Expanding your horizons will help you get out of your comfort zone with the knock-on effect of boosting your self-esteem. That someone special may not be in the class itself, but by widening your circle of friends, invitations will follow that could lead to unexpected new connections.

2 **Festivals**
The spring and summer months are full of festivals—music, cookery, literary, and historical. Go along with a like-minded friend and sign up to any events taking place, perhaps a book signing or a cookery class. Start up a conversation with someone else while standing in line and who knows where it might lead.

3 **Volunteering**
Getting involved and helping out with something you care about is a great way to keep the mind active, but also widens the opportunity to meet someone new. There's a wide range of volunteering opportunities available, whether it's committing to a local cause or a larger national charity, and the work is rewarding in itself.

4 **Meet-ups**
Meetup.com is a social networking site that allows you to find and join groups related to your own personal interests and activities, and then to arrange to meet up in person at meetings in your area. There are a number already in existence and you can sign up and start your own meet-up group wherever you live.

5 **Take up a new sport**
This is a win-win choice, as you'll find opportunities to meet new people and keep yourself fit at the same time, which is a great confidence booster for when you do go on a date. Think of something you'd like to try that might interest like-minded people whether it be golf, swimming, or joining a gym.

6 **Online dating**
There's a huge choice of online dating sites available and the stigma of finding love in this way has completely disappeared. It's perfectly normal, and extremely common, to find couples who have met online. You can take your time, browsing at your leisure and start a conversation from the comfort of your own home. You can then take things at your own pace and later ensure you arrange to meet in a busy, public place. So what are you waiting for?

"Have enough courage to trust love one more time and always one more time"

MAYA ANGELOU

Voyage of rediscovery

Whether it's a book first read as a child or a song first heard as a teenager, chancing upon an old favorite brings with it the opportunity to share cultural memories with friends and family

Rediscovering a pleasure can bring real delight. It could be as simple as finding a well-worn paperback on a shelf of newer books. There's something appealing about its creased spine and a flicker of recognition ignites. Perhaps on closer view, it's a classic novel, a book from your childhood that provided a gateway to a magical land, or Antoine de Saint-Exupéry's *The Little Prince*, a tale that offered a philosophical glimpse into the behavior of grown-ups. Rediscovery can be an invitation to reminisce over who you once were and an opportunity to evaluate who you've become since.

Like the bookshelf find, the rediscovery may come about as a surprise. It can also be something sought out. A nostalgic chat with friends about Gabriel Axel's 1987 classic, *Babette's Feast*, could see you downloading the movie to assess once more Stéphane Audran's performance in the titular role, or a documentary about early science-fiction programs might lead you to check out William Shatner in the early *Star Trek* series (made all the easier with technology and numerous channels, but you might need to resist the temptation to binge-watch).

New and old approaches

YouTube also offers immediate opportunities. You can transport yourself back to live recordings of David Bowie's *Space Oddity* while music-streaming services make finding obscure tracks and long-forgotten artists immediately accessible. Downloading a Chet Baker or Billie Holiday song might have you dancing in the kitchen or move you to tears. And if you can't stream or download, a quick online search on a phone can see the item swiftly ordered and delivered.

It doesn't have to be this way of course. An old-school approach may be the only way if what you're looking for is not readily available. For many, the search is part of the joy. Consider looking for a long-lost edition of a particular book or record that may have been, in retrospect, recklessly discarded—the newer versions don't hold the same appeal. Calling up or visiting secondhand bookstores and hearing the good news—"yes, we have it"—or finding Kraftwerk's 1977 album, *Trans-Europe Express*, (which led to your love of electronica and house music) in a box of recently donated LPs in a thrift store, can be hugely gratifying.

Nostalgic journeys

Rediscovery can even make time-travel seem possible and take you back to an era when you may have been a very different person. Listening again to an album played regularly in your college dorm could prompt memories of independence, friendships you thought would last forever, and nights out on a student budget. Those days might be over, but it doesn't mean you can't savor the feelings again. A particular song might even provide inspiration to search for one of those long-lost roommates. Rediscovery can involve more than unearthing a book or board game, and social media makes it that bit easier to reconnect with old friends. Who knows, you might even decide to meet up again if there are still common shared interests (or you'll decide after a few posts or emails that the relationship is best left in the past).

Does it still hold the same appeal?

Similar feelings can arise when you embark on other forms of rediscovery. Is it as good as you remembered or better than the first time? Do you recall the ending or how the plot twists and turns? Do the lyrics still move you? Does the lead actor still make your heart beat faster or has their charm faded with time? It may be you're able

"Distance not only gives nostalgia, but perspective, and maybe objectivity"

ROBERT MORGAN

to appreciate your rediscovery in a different way now or that it's lost its appeal completely. The only way to find out is to re-experience it.

This time round, try to savor that rediscovered children's classic, TV series, or album. Take it slowly. Let's take that once-loved book: Become immersed in the writing, try to pick up on any subtle nuances or messages you might have missed as a child; look beyond the story and get lost in the detail and sequence of the words; ask if your life experiences have made it easier to understand a character's motivation. A fresh assessment might prompt a desire to read other books from the author's oeuvre.

Or the opposite could be true. A TV series you once considered the funniest of all time, for instance, might now seem horribly outdated and barely raise a smile.

Sharing your finds

One of the most rewarding aspects of rediscovery is sharing what you've found with friends and family. Finding an old train set in the attic and inviting children (young and older) to help set it up (and to play) is an invitation to everyone to share in a fun experience. Similarly, a younger person's enthusiasm for a reworked or closely derived classic movie can be the ideal opportunity to pass on the original and for you both to sit down and compare the two. How does 2016's romantic musical *La La Land* stand up to 1935's *Top Hat* or 1952's *Singin' in the Rain*? And who's the best dancer? Sharing your rediscoveries can foster closer relationships and new experiences. Who knows, perhaps your favorite movie or book could become part of someone's else's history?

REDISCOVERY GAME

Imagine you were going to be cast away forever on a remote desert island—and you had to choose just one recording, one book, and one luxury item to take with you. Your choices should be linked to your past or bring back memories that are particularly heartfelt or meaningful.

In the space below, write a shortlist of 12 items from which to choose your must-have items. You could have four books, four movies, and four recordings (these could be songs, a radio sketch, sports commentary, a reading of a much-loved poem) but mix it up to suit your life.

Give real thought to what you want on the list and why. Then write down your final 12 here. . .

1 ....

2 ....

3 ....

4 ....

5 ....

6 ....

7 ....

8 ....

9 ....

10 ....

11 ....

12 ....

Now it's time to get really engaged. Seek out your choices. Download them or research where you might find them. Then take the opportunity to immerse yourself in your rediscoveries. Consider the following:

- Have your choices stood the test of time?
- What memories have been evoked?
- Do you have an altered appreciation now you're at a different point of your life?
- Are there details that you didn't notice first time around?
- Are there any particular choices that you'd like to share with others so they, too, can share in your enthusiasm?

If you really enjoy the experience, you might want to invite friends and family members to try it, too, and then discuss what's on their list and why it's important. Memories, significant moments, and cultural treats are all there to be shared.

Taste of *life*

Turn up your sense of taste to enjoy delicious, nutritious meals for optimum good health

If you were to conduct a snap poll around a table of diners, you might find they had a range of differing relationships with the food they were eating. Some people live to eat, and some eat to live. The foodies at the table would likely pore over the dish in front of them and take great pleasure in what they were eating and its aromas, flavors, and textures. Others might simply see food as a fuel for their bodies to work efficiently and effectively, eating quickly with very little connection to the food on their plates.

Whatever relationship you have with food as you grow up, being mindful of what you eat as you start to age is essential for good health, particularly as your keen sense of taste may diminish over time. Whether you have always been a gourmand who relishes every morsel you eat or someone who sticks to eating the same dishes week in and week out, being aware of the need to entice your taste buds with tempting food will ensure you have a nutritious diet—and this plays a crucial role in keeping well as you get older.

How we taste

The sensation of taste is the receptor cells (or taste buds) in your mouth coming into contact with molecules in the food and drink you consume and sending signals to your brain. This triggers a chemical reaction that, in combination with smell, allows you to perceive flavors. The tongue is covered with thousands of small visible bumps (called papillae), each containing hundreds of taste buds. There are approximately 5,000 taste buds on the tongue, with more on the roof, sides, and back of the mouth and in the throat. Each taste bud contains 50 to 100 taste receptor cells.

These cells detect the five basic flavors of sweet, salty, sour, bitter, and savory. Other factors contributing to enjoyment of food include texture, temperature, and coolness (like menthol) or hotness (a vindaloo curry, for example), which are detected through different receptors.

Changes with age

Research has indicated that taste perception can decline as people get older, because of a decrease in the number of taste buds and shrinkage of remaining ones. Your mouth also produces less saliva, which can affect your sense of taste. Reduced sensitivity to the five tastes often occurs after the age of 60. One study, published in the journal *Chemical Sciences*, found that older people had less sensitivity to salty and sweet flavors especially.

A diminishing sense of smell can also reduce the ability to detect flavors. Other things—like smoking, certain medications, and some diseases—can also affect your senses and therefore your enjoyment of food.

Aging is not the only contributor to diminished interest in food, explains Ngaire Hobbins, a dietitian, author, and international authority on nutrition for older adults. "It's also related to life events, illness, and loss, medication interaction and having inadequate access to appealing, nutritionally adequate or age-appropriate food," she says.

Losing interest in food can do more than interfere with your enjoyment of eating. In her booklet *Nutrition For Seniors*, Ngaire explains that malnutrition can occur when you don't eat enough of the right foods, so your body doesn't get the nutrients it needs.

She explains that malnutrition is a common cause of poor health in older adults, and can contribute to infection, falls, confusion, rapid physical and cognitive decline, and even premature death. The most common sign of malnutrition is weight loss, especially if it is rapid and unintentional. It is also possible to be overweight and malnourished. Other signs include feeling tired all the time, loss of strength, poor concentration, slow wound healing, and difficulty recovering from illnesses, Ngaire writes.

"This is my invariable advice to people: Learn how to cook—try new recipes, learn from your mistakes, be fearless, and above all have fun!"

JULIA CHILD

But there's some good news. Ngaire says: "The vast majority of people now in their late 60s and beyond continue to relish opportunities to share meals with friends and family, and enjoy food just as they always have. In fact, they have the advantage of having had the very best nutritional start in life—eating fresh, seasonal and local food, leading active lives, and working hard to avoid wasting any morsel on offer."

Spice things up

Adding a bit of salt or sugar, along with various herbs, some spices, and/or condiments, can really aid a person's enjoyment of their meal—especially for those who might feel their appreciation of food is starting to wane. "The salt or sugar may not be great for people in their 40s or 50s with often the same number of years ahead of them, but in later life it's more important to enjoy meals, and flagging tastebuds sometimes need help."

She suggests amping up the flavor of dishes with the likes of garlic, onion, ginger, and pepper. Try cooking with wine or acidic flavors such as citrus and vinegar, or adding a scoop of natural or Greek-style yogurt to your recipes.

Ngaire adds that as people move into their 80s, 90s, and beyond, "they can afford (unlike those of us who are younger), to embrace a few more treats."

The appeal of food

Another way to increase enjoyment of eating is sharing meals with others. "Loneliness and isolation kill appetites and snatch away enjoyment, so eating well is often about social activities," Ngaire says. Try cooking with or for friends and family. Experiment with new cookery books or recipes from magazines if you feel the need for inspiration, or cook up an old favorite and enjoy reminiscing about earlier times.

While taste buds might diminish, people also eat with their eyes, Ngaire says in her guide. The way food is presented can make it more (or less) appealing. Don't forget to add color and texture to your plate. This not only increases the number of vitamins and minerals, but makes food look and taste better.

It can also be wise to visit your doctor to rule out any medical causes for a loss of appetite, especially if you have had rapid or unexplained weight loss. If you're a smoker, quitting can help to restore enjoyment of food.

Healthy choices

Ngaire notes that eating well is key to getting the most out of your senior years. She recommends including a protein-rich food at the center of every meal, surrounded by a wide variety of different colored vegetables, fruits, nuts, seeds, and grains. Eat a rainbow! Add a healthy oil (from olives, nuts, or seeds) and as many herbs and spices as you like.

"The protein supports the essential muscle reserve which underpins immune capacity, body organ maintenance, wound repair, and brain fuel supply," she says. "Colored foods provide antioxidant and anti-inflammatory substances to protect cells in the body and brain."

Getting older might mean the taste buds don't work as well as they used to, but it doesn't have to spell the end of your love of food. Putting a few simple strategies in place can ensure you continue to get pleasure out of eating, plus the nutrients you need to fuel a healthy body and mind.

MINDFUL EATING

Mindful eating can help to address unhealthy food behaviors, like eating too quickly or too much. It is about being present in the moment, celebrating the joy and satisfaction of eating, without judging or criticizing yourself

Tips for mindful eating from Jean Hailes for *Women's Health*

1 Start slowly. Choose one meal per day to eat more mindfully. If that seems too much of a shift, start with eating one meal per week.

2 Before eating, check in with how you're feeling. Are you hungry, thirsty, stressed, bored, or rushed? You may be able to identify whether certain emotions compel you to eat—comfort or distraction eating, for example. Tune in to your body.

3 Turn off distractions. Switch off the TV and mute your cell phone notifications to put the focus on enjoying your meal and your own company, or that of the people around you.

4 Keep serving bowls and leftovers off the table, so your focus is on the plate directly in front of you.

5 Slow down and notice the colors, flavors, and textures of your food. Chew slowly and pause between each mouthful. Aim to take about 20 minutes to eat a meal.

6 Think about the journey your food took to get to your plate. Gratitude and appreciation can add enjoyment to your experience.

7 Make it a habit. Download the mindful eating poster from Jean Hailes (jeanhailes.org.au) and put it somewhere that will remind you to slow down and savor your food.

DIFFERENT SEASONS

Salt and pepper are often the standard condiments used to flavor food, but with a fresh approach, a bit of imagination, and some zingy spices you can really get the taste buds firing again. Here, acclaimed chef Nik Sharma shares three recipes that do just that

---

CRAB CAKES WITH LEMONGRASS AND GREEN MANGO

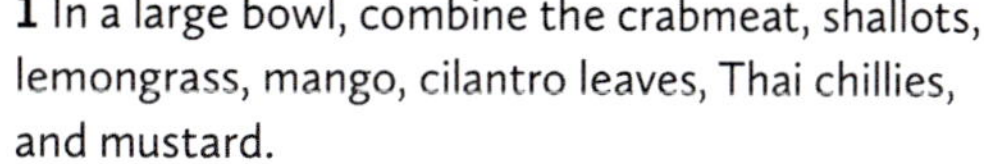

My mom loved crab cakes so much she'd sometimes lose count as she made batch after batch. I'd take advantage of the abundance and sneak one away every time I walked through the kitchen. She never said a word, but she must have known what was going on. What makes these crab cakes stand out is the combination of hot and sour flavors from the minced Thai chillies and bits of fresh green mango. I usually use equal parts of lump and back fin.

MAKES 7 APPETIZER SERVINGS

- 16 oz (455g) fresh crabmeat
- 4 shallots, minced
- 2 tbsp minced lemongrass (white part only)
- 3 tbsp finely diced fresh green mango
- 2 tbsp fresh cilantro leaves
- 2 Thai chillies, seeded, if desired, and minced
- 1 tbsp Dijon mustard
- 1 tsp coriander seeds
- 1 tsp garam masala
- 1 whole lime, plus 2 limes, cut into wedges (optional)
- ½ tsp fine sea salt
- ½ cup (35g) dry breadcrumbs
- 2 large egg yolks
- Vegetable oil for frying

1 In a large bowl, combine the crabmeat, shallots, lemongrass, mango, cilantro leaves, Thai chillies, and mustard.

2 Using a mortar and pestle or spice grinder, grind the coriander seeds to a coarse powder and add to the crabmeat with the garam masala.

3 Grate the lime zest and juice the whole lime. Add 1 tsp of the zest and 1 tbsp of the juice to the crabmeat, discarding the remaining zest and juice.

4 Add the salt and breadcrumbs and mix gently to combine. Add the egg yolks and fold it into the crabmeat mixture.

5 Divide the mixture into 14 equal parts and shape into 2 in (5cm) rounds, 1 in (2.5cm) thick.

6 Heat 1 to 1½ tbsp of oil in a medium cast-iron or nonstick skillet over a medium to low heat. Place four cakes in the skillet and cook until golden brown and crispy—between 2½ and 3 minutes on each side.

7 Drain on paper towels.

8 Transfer to a plate and serve with the lime wedges.

NAAN

MAKES 4 FLATBREADS

I prefer homemade naan to the dense and doughy store-bought ones. It's easy to whip up. You just need to plan ahead so the dough has time to rise. I use wholewheat pastry flour to make naan because it contains more fiber than all-purpose flour but less gluten, which helps produce a softer bread. While the choice of toppings is endless, the margherita pizza (see opposite page), sprinkled with nigella seeds, is my favorite way to eat up the colorful little tomatoes that grow in our backyard.

- ½ cup (120ml) whole milk, heated to 105-115°F (41-46°C)
- 1 large egg
- 2 tbsp plain full-fat Greek yogurt
- 1 tbsp unsalted butter, melted
- 1 tbsp sugar
- 1 tsp fine sea salt
- 1 tbsp active dry yeast
- 2½ cups (280g) all-purpose flour or wholewheat pastry flour, plus more for rolling out the naans

1 Using a fork, whisk the milk, egg, yogurt, butter, sugar, and salt in a small bowl.

2 Sprinkle with the yeast and let sit for 5 minutes. The mixture should be bubbly on the surface.

3 Put the flour in a large bowl or mound on a clean work surface and make a well in the center. Pour the yeast mixture into the middle. Using clean hands or a large wooden spoon, gradually mix the flour from the inside wall of the well into the liquid to form a sticky dough. Knead well for 4 to 5 minutes.

4 Fold the dough by grabbing it from the underside and stretching it and folding it back over itself.

5 Rotate a quarter of a turn and repeat 3 or 4 times.

6 Brush a large bowl with a little oil and put the dough in the bowl. Cover with plastic wrap and allow to rise in a dark, warm place until doubled in size (approximately 4 hours).

7 Divide the dough into four equal parts and shape into balls (or as specified by your recipe). On a clean, lightly floured work surface, use a rolling pin to roll out the balls of dough, one at a time, into circles about ⅛ in. (4mm) thick and about 6 in. (15cm) in diameter.

8 To cook the naan, heat a large, lidded skillet over a medium to high heat. Place a circle of dough into the hot skillet and cover to trap the steam. Cook for 3 to 4 minutes, flip the dough, and turn the heat to low. Cook, covered, until the naan blisters, with a few big bubbles (1 to 2 minutes). Remove from the pan and wrap in kitchen towel. Repeat with the remaining three circles of dough.

GHEE

MAKES APPROXIMATELY 1 CUP (250G)

Ghee is one of the most popular fats used in Indian cooking. It is a form of clarified butter, from which the milk solids and water are removed. Because the milk solids and sugars are caramelized in the fat before their removal, they give the ghee a nutty fragrance. Ghee can last for months if stored correctly because the water, sugar, and proteins are all removed.

- 2 cups (455g) unsalted butter, cubed

1 Line a strainer with a few layers of cheesecloth and place over a clean, dry 2 cup (480ml) jar with a tight-fitting lid to hold the finished ghee. Set aside.

2 In a heavy, medium saucepan over a medium to high heat, melt the butter, stirring occasionally with a large metal spoon. As the butter melts, skim off and discard any foam that rises to the surface.

3 Cook until all the water in the butter boils off and the fat stops sizzling and turns a deep-golden yellow. The milk solids at the bottom of the saucepan will be reddish-brown. The entire process should take between 12 and 15 minutes.

4 Remove the saucepan from the heat and carefully pour the liquid through the cheesecloth-lined strainer into the jar.

5 Seal the jar and store the ghee in a cool, dark place for up to 3 months in the refrigerator.

MARGHERITA NAAN PIZZA

MAKES 2 INDIVIDUAL PIZZAS

- Dough of 1 recipe naan (see opposite page)
- 2 tsp all-purpose flour, plus more for rolling out the pizza
- 2 tsp coriander seeds
- 2 tsp nigella seeds
- 2 tsp dried red chilli flakes
- 2 tsp cornmeal or semolina
- 4 tbsp (50g) ghee (see opposite page), melted
- 6½ oz (185g) cherry tomatoes, halved crosswise
- 5½ oz (160g) grape tomatoes, halved lengthwise
- 3 oz (80g) shredded mozzarella
- 1 tbsp chopped fresh chives
- 1 tbsp flaky sea salt

1 Place a baking steel or pizza stone on a rack in the middle of the oven and preheat the oven to 500°F (260°C) for 30 minutes.

2 Divide the dough into two equal parts and shape into balls. Cover one ball with a kitchen towel.

3 On a clean, lightly floured work surface, roll the other ball into a circle ⅛ in. (4mm) thick and 12 in. (30cm) in diameter. Cover loosely with a kitchen towel. Repeat with the second ball of dough.

4 Crack the coriander lightly with a mortar and pestle, add the nigella seeds and chilli flakes, then set aside.

5 Prepare one pizza at a time: Flip over a baking sheet, wrong-side up, and place a sheet of parchment paper on the baking sheet.

6 Sprinkle 1 tsp of the flour and 1 tsp of the cornmeal on the parchment to coat evenly.

7 Place a rolled-out circle of dough on top of the paper and drizzle with a little melted ghee.

8 Spread half of the tomatoes over the dough. Sprinkle with half the mozzarella and 1 tbsp of the spices from the mortar.

9 Slide the circle of dough onto the preheated baking steel, discard the parchment paper, and shut the oven door.

10 Lower the heat to 425°F (220°C) and bake until the edges of the crust start to turn golden (between 10 and 12 minutes).

11 Garnish with half the chopped chives and flaky salt, and drizzle with a little extra ghee. Repeat with the remaining circle of dough and serve the pizzas hot.

"Every tradition had to begin somewhere at some point, so go ahead and break the rules and make your own traditions!"

NIK SHARMA

Edited extract from *Season* by Nik Sharma, Chronicle Books, £26. Photographs: Nik Sharma

DATE AND TAMARIND LOAF

The inspiration for this cake is a sweet chutney made from dates and tamarind, which is commonly served as a dipping sauce with samosas and other fried snacks. I often dust this cake with powdered sugar or drizzle it with crème fraîche.

MAKES 8 TO 9 SERVINGS (ONE 8½ IN. [21.5CM] LOAF)

- 3 oz (90g) sour tamarind pulp or paste
- 1 cup (240ml) boiling water
- 2½ cups (280g) all-purpose flour
- 2 tsp ground ginger
- ½ tsp freshly ground black pepper
- 1½ tsp baking powder
- ½ tsp baking soda
- ¼ tsp fine sea salt
- 16 pitted Medjool dates, finely chopped
- ½ cup (60g) chopped walnuts, plus 6 walnut halves
- ¾ cup (180ml), plus 1 tsp extra-virgin olive oil
- ¾ cup (150g) packed jaggery or muscovado sugar
- 2 large eggs, at room temperature
- 1 cup (120g) powdered sugar

1 Put the tamarind in a medium heat-proof bowl and add the boiling water, pressing down on the tamarind with a spoon so it's covered with water. Cover with plastic wrap and let sit for at least 1 hour.

2 Massage and squeeze the pulp to soften it, then press through a fine-mesh strainer suspended over a bowl, discarding the solids in the strainer.

3 Measure out 8½ oz (240g) pulp for this recipe. Reserve 2 tbsp of the pulp in a small bowl to prepare the glaze.

4 Preheat the oven to 350°F (180°C) and grease a 8½x4½ in (21.5x11cm) loaf pan with butter (line the bottom with parchment paper).

5 In a large bowl, whisk together the flour, ginger, pepper, baking powder, baking soda, and salt.

6 Put the dates in a small bowl. Add the chopped walnuts and 2 tbsp of the whisked dry ingredients and toss to coat evenly.

7 Combine ¾ cup (180ml) olive oil and the jaggery or muscovado sugar in a blender. Pulse on high speed for a few seconds until completely emulsified.

8 Add 1 egg and pulse for 3 to 4 seconds, until combined. Repeat with the remaining egg.

9 Make a well in the center of the dry ingredients in the bowl and pour the egg mixture into the well. Whisk the dry ingredients into the egg mixture and continue whisking until there are no visible flecks of flour remaining. Then fold in the dates and chopped walnuts.

10 Spoon the batter into the prepared loaf pan. Arrange the walnuts halves in a straight line down the center of the loaf.

11 Bake for 55 to 60 minutes, rotating the pan halfway through baking, until firm to the touch in the center and a skewer comes out clean.

12 Cool in the loaf pan on a wire rack for about 10 minutes. When ready, run a knife around the inside of the pan to release the cake. Remove from the loaf pan and transfer to a wire rack to cool completely.

13 Add the remaining 1 tsp of olive oil to the small bowl containing the reserved tamarind. Sift in the powdered sugar and whisk until completely smooth. Pour the glaze over the cooled loaf and let it sit for 1 hour to set before serving.

From solitude to loneliness

Spending time on your own has many positive aspects, but there may be instances when you find yourself feeling isolated. Here's how to stay engaged with the world and keep loneliness at bay

Whether you're someone who loves the company of others or who's perfectly happy spending an afternoon without the need to engage in conversation, you may experience times when you feel the need to retreat and recharge your batteries. Sometimes craving solitude and spending time alone can be restorative and a useful form of self-care.

Other times, being alone is not a luxury but can cross over into something almost punitive, when loneliness seeps in and a yearning to connect with others takes hold. There are subtle differences between choosing downtime alone and the basic human need for connection with others. Keeping those often nuanced differences in check can help prevent loneliness from developing into a number of chronic health conditions, including depression.

When loneliness develops

Some people describe themselves as feeling lonely because they don't see or talk to anyone very often, others are surrounded by people, but they don't feel understood or cared for.

Loneliness can hit at any time of life—those who spend much of their time hiding behind their computer screens and on social media are vulnerable to being affected by missing out on essential face-to-face time with their peers. New moms can feel isolated and alone when looking after their babies.

And it's little wonder that, when you stop working, you can start to feel isolated and disengaged from life. After years of being physically so close to others on a day-to-day basis—sometimes getting on with colleagues and sometimes not—having no one to bat ideas off or spark up a conversation with about last night's TV or a new movie release can take time to accept. For many, self-esteem is inexorably linked to their career status, and without a job to use as a hook, you can find yourself retreating from the wider world, fearing you have nothing to offer. Before you know it, that initial withdrawal can lead to isolation and loneliness.

Empty nesters can often experience similar feelings of worthlessness, when their role as care-giver has gone. Their identity and sense of being needed, so wrapped up in the regular grind of looking after children, is left wanting. When these landmark events happen, it's important to stay active and engaged to prevent loneliness from taking hold.

Plenty of research has shown the harm of social isolation, sometimes considered a public health risk in countries with aging populations. The number of Americans aged 65 and older is projected to more than double from 46 million in 2015 to over 98 million by 2060, and the 65-and-older age group's share of the total population will rise to nearly 24 percent from 15 percent.

How personality can invite loneliness

Strong social connections are considered important not just for cognitive and motor functions, but also the immune system. Their absence is particularly acute in cases of extreme isolation, when prolonged confinement and solitude can lead to forms of mental instability. But these are severe and involuntary cases of aloneness.

"There is a solitude, which each and every one of us has always carried with him, more inaccessible than the ice-cold mountains, more profound than the midnight sea; the solitude of self"

ELIZABETH CADY STANTON

Many people just prefer plenty of alone time, which has a number of positive aspects, such as improved creativity and focus, and fewer but stronger friendships.

If you are someone who is more prone to loneliness than others—the type of person who may well be something of a perfectionist, or who without making a fuss just gets on with life, sometimes working too hard and submerging yourself in or hiding behind your career, and you're more introverted in your nature—there's more of a chance you can convince yourself you're always happier on your own. The danger is that when you then spend too much time in solitude, you may find it almost impossible to break free from your aloneness and get back out into the world.

That invitation from a friend to coffee, the weekly meeting of your local campaign group, the regular trips to galleries and exhibitions—all these ways of engaging gradually become too taxing and full of potential risk for those who seek safety alone. It is then that time alone segues into social isolation.

Talk about how you're feeling

Loneliness still seems to be one of the last taboos in society. Many people will more easily admit to feeling depressed than lonely. There's a stigma attached and you may fear you'll be judged—as unlikable or not worthy of having friends—and find it hard to talk about your sense of aloneness, alienation, or exclusion.

And not being able to talk about your feelings can compound the problem as your isolation becomes a self-fulfilling prophecy. If you judge yourself to be lonely, you may be giving yourself negative messages of unworthiness, making it more difficult to take steps to change the situation.

It's important to remember that loneliness is often caused by loss—of loved ones, a sociable workplace, or self-esteem, for example—and that if you're feeling lonely, it's not your fault.

Consider also that it's not unusual to feel this way. A 2018 study of 20,000 US adults revealed that nearly half of people suffer from feelings of loneliness.

The evaluation found that nearly half of Americans report sometimes or always feeling alone (46 percent) or left out (47 percent).

There are people who can offer help, but only if you let them know. Going to your doctor is a good place to start and they can direct you to services for support.

Plan ahead

If you are someone who suddenly finds that a week can go by and you haven't seen anyone, it's important to plan ahead. Making sure there are activities penciled in your diary in advance will ensure that your month has been arranged, and that you have connections with others on a regular basis.

For instance, if Easter is a particularly difficult time, check out which of your friends and acquaintances will also be at a loose end, and make arrangements to meet. It won't stop you from being alone, but knowing you have plans later in the day will keep you from being lonely.

Always connect

However much you convince yourself that you enjoy your own company, if you have feelings of loneliness it could well be your body telling you that you need more social contact. Finding ways to meet more, or different, people will help ease such emotions and improve your outlook on life as you start to connect and make new, fulfilling relationships.

WAYS TO ENGAGE

Turn to your local community to break feelings of loneliness

Take up a new activity

Visit your library or community center to find out what local activities may be of interest. Joining a walking group will provide exercise as well as social interaction. There are a wide range of activities to get involved in, from dancing and cookery classes to walking clubs and art groups, to combat loneliness.
See what courses are on offer at your local adult education center. Brush up on existing skills or try something out of your comfort zone, like a new language, or a science subject such as astronomy.

Volunteer

If you've recently retired and have more time on your hands, volunteering is a great way to get involved and engage. The social aspects are as important for most volunteers as the work they are doing, and many find the time spent in their chosen field extremely fulfilling. There's a huge choice available from working in historical buildings or the countryside to helping with animals or young children. Check out local charities to see if they are looking for volunteers or search online.

ONE FOR THE ROAD

Whether you want to tour Switzerland by train or soak up the culture of Málaga, the opportunities for traveling solo are plentiful and just waiting to be explored

Traveling alone, especially on vacation, can seem a daunting prospect if you've never done it before. It may be that you're no longer part of a couple, or that your usual travel companion is unable to accompany you. But if you want to go on vacation, or just feel the need for a break, why deny yourself?

Whether you're experiencing a life change following divorce or bereavement, or if you feel you'd simply rather go away on your own, a solo trip can be a confidence booster and give you the courage to try all sorts of other new things. And if you have recently lost a partner, visiting somewhere new—without memories of previous visits together—can be helpful.

If you're new to traveling alone and not sure how you'll feel about it, try a mini-break first. It could be just a couple of days somewhere not too far from home or a short trip to a different state—if you feel comfortable with that, then you can plan a longer trip.

Some people feel happier traveling with a group where everything is arranged, but beware of ending up on a tour that is full of couples—and you. There are numerous singles resorts these days or you could look into booking a train trip or a cruise. A number of cruise companies, such as Fred Olsen, cater for solo travelers. This is especially attractive if you don't like flying or are used to flying with a companion who would normally be able to distract you from feeling anxious.

Alternatively, if you like to have more freedom and the chance to be spontaneous, think about hiring a car, especially if you plan on visiting more than one place. For example, Ortigia in Syracuse is a beautiful place to stay on Sicily's rugged south-east coast, but it would be a shame to miss the charms of baroque towns such as Noto and Ragusa. If you have a car, not only can you sidestep waiting around for public transport, but you can also be impulsive if you feel the urge to get out and explore. You'll need to be a fairly confident driver, but if you're comfortable driving on this trip, then you may find yourself ready to plan your next one.

Doing some kind of activity on vacation might be a good idea if you can't think how you'll fill your time on your own. There are lots of different kinds available: Cooking, walking, painting, learning a language, cycling, yoga—basically, pick an activity and somewhere you'd like to go, then see if you can pair the two. They may or may not be aimed at singles but chances are, if you've chosen a vacation doing something you enjoy, you'll meet like-minded people.

Another way to ease yourself into traveling alone is to start or end the trip with a short visit to friends or family. You may know someone who lives in, say, southern Spain, who has previously invited you to visit but you don't want to impose for more than a couple of days. By beginning your holiday with them, it will act as a bit of a buffer, and your hosts can give you some tips on places to visit. Then you could spend a week or two relaxing at a beach resort or enjoying tapas and culture—the city of Málaga alone has around 40 museums.

There are also lots of ways to receive support and stay in touch with friends and family when you're traveling alone. You might want to keep in contact by sending a daily email about what you've been up to, connecting

"To awaken quite alone in a strange town is one of the pleasantest sensations in the world"

FREYA STARK

TOP TIPS

- Try a short break first if you're not sure how you'll feel about traveling alone. If you enjoy it, plan a longer vacation as soon as you get home.
- Don't go on a group tour that is going to consist of all couples and you. There are lots of vacations aimed at single travelers (of all ages, or 55+ if you prefer), from cruises to skiing—or just loafing around at a cozy hotel.
- If you think you'll feel uncomfortable eating alone, try having your main meal at lunchtime rather than in the evening.
- Try to speak a little of the language if you're abroad, or at the very least have a phrasebook handy. It's hard enough being lost for words when you're with a companion, but when you're on your own you'll feel really isolated.
- If you don't want to spend a lot of time alone, an activity vacation will introduce you to people with similar interests, and also give you a structure to the day.
- Try to do as much planning and research as possible before your vacation—that way, you're more likely to be able to relax and enjoy yourself once you're there.

through FaceTime or Skype, or simply post pictures of your trip on social media (no, you're not too old—if William Shatner, 87, is on Instagram, you can be, too). And if you have a dog, you could consider taking your pet along with you—not only will it be familiar company but, as many dog owners will attest, it's a sure-fire way of breaking the ice and meeting new people.

Planning your trip in advance can be just as enjoyable as organizing a trip with a partner, especially if you see it as a chance to indulge yourself. It's a good idea to think ahead, to minimize any anxiety you might have when you're away. If you get an early flight and have booked a hotel room, remember you may not be able to check in until later. And if you book a late flight, think about how you're going to spend the time until you need to be at the airport—and the possibility of delays scuppering plans. Flights at a more civilized hour can be expensive, but it may be worth it if you avoid being tired or anxious.

Also, think carefully about your destination. Two major considerations for solo travelers are staying safe and not feeling that you're being penalized because you're alone. Because solo travel has increased in recent years, having to pay a single supplement isn't always an issue, especially if you're staying somewhere that charges per person rather than per room. But if there's a supplement and you're unwilling to pay it, there are ways around it. If you don't travel in high season, you may be able to negotiate a better rate—or think about renting a small apartment through a site such as Airbnb.

And finally—one of the great pleasures about being on vacation is to try new cafés and restaurants, but how do you feel about eating alone if you're not used to it? Even though you know others won't bat an eyelid at the sight of a solo diner, you may still be feeling a little conspicuous—but you can make it easier. For a start, you'll probably feel more comfortable having a casual lunch alone rather than a formal evening meal. Some people prefer to sit at the bar rather than at a table for one. Bring a book or a magazine, or use the time to make plans for the following day—who knows, if you're scribbling furiously in a notebook you may be mistaken for a restaurant critic and given five-star treatment.

DESTINATIONS TO CONSIDER

Lisbon / Sintra, Portugal Portugal's capital, Lisbon, is a relatively small city and you can pack a lot into a few days—riding the city's famous trams, a pastel de nata (or four), and Sintra's fairy-tale palaces (a short train-ride away).

Lake District, UK Whether you're joining a walking group or enjoying one of the area's Michelin-starred restaurants, the views are stunning all year round—many hotels do special seasonal packages, including trips and activities which you can drop in and out of. The combination of hikers and tourists generally makes it a friendly, buzzy place.

Japan (*pictured top*) Solo travelers often rate Japan as a particularly safe place to visit, and as many hotels charge per person, not per room, single supplement isn't an issue. If your trip coincides with cherry blossom season, that's a bonus, but don't bank on it being perfectly on time—unlike the trains.

Crete, Greece A vacation on the largest of the Greek islands can be as sociable as you want it to be. Do your own thing—or try the Mistral hotel in Maleme, which is specifically aimed at solo travelers of all ages.

Biking in Italy Activities are ideal if you don't want to sightsee solo. Join an organized biking tour in a beautiful setting such as Lake Garda—and if you'd rather take it easy, hire an e-bike. If you do want to do some sightseeing, work in a trip to nearby Verona.

Northern Spain If you want an adventure but don't want to head too far off the beaten track, visit the beautiful Cantabrian coast.

Vienna, Austria (*pictured below*) With a packed itinerary of museums, art galleries, and Sachertorte, a traveling companion would just slow you down as you explore Austria's cultured capital. Even a coffee in Café Landtmann has an almost laughably rich history, with Freud, Klimt, and Mahler among its previous customers.

Sicily, Italy The baroque towns of south-east Sicily offer a feast for the eyes as well as the stomach. Ragusa and Noto are highlights, with the latter laying claim to the best ice-cream in Sicily—some say, the world. Planning your own itinerary is half the fun, and hiring a car allows you to be spontaneous.

Train tour in Switzerland There are a number of recommended routes to take, and you can customize them and make them as long or short as you like. The scenery is the real star here.

BRAIN POWER

Continue looking after the gray matter to get the most out of life

Dispel any myth that memory loss is an inevitable part of the aging process. As the birthdays pass, it might take a little longer to remember where you've left your glasses, the password to your email account, or what you rushed upstairs for, but this is seldom a cause for concern. Humans produce new brain cells throughout their lives, so while forgetfulness may be frustrating at times, your brain is still capable of great knowledge and wisdom. All you need to do is protect your gray matter by eating a well-balanced diet, exercising body and mind, and spending time socializing and engaging with people whose company you enjoy.

Adopting healthy lifestyle habits and maintaining them is the first step. Stick to a wholesome diet to optimize your brain's health and keep it active and alert, fruit and vegetables are great basic staples. Add blueberries, blackberries, and raspberries to your shopping cart. They're all packed with antioxidants and, if eaten regularly, along with dark leafy greens, such as kale and spinach, and cruciferous veg, perhaps broccoli, cabbage, or cauliflower, they'll help to provide the brain with memory-boosting vitamins and nutrients. Food high in omega-3 fatty acids, like salmon, sardines, and walnuts, are also useful for a sharp mind.

Physical activity is pivotal, too. During exercise, chemicals are released that stimulate the hippocampus, the part of the brain that's largely responsible for memory. Embark on a daily swim, gym session, or even a brisk 30-minute walk and your brain is sure to benefit, as well as your whole well-being.

Mentally challenging pastimes will also give the muscles in your brain a good workout. Attempt the crossword in a newspaper, try a Sudoku, or download brain-training apps—you'll find plenty of word games, number pattern bafflers, and memory teasers online. Just make sure the puzzles are tough enough, because those that are too easy won't do as much to keep your mind fighting fit.

You may want to experiment with activities that require manual dexterity, such as drawing, coloring, or craftwork. Or why not learn a new language? Not only is this a tonic for the brain, research suggests it also helps to improve verbal fluency and intelligence. Writing in a diary or journal is another way to keep language skills intact, especially if you push yourself to write in a creative, descriptive way, using words that are not normally in your vocabulary.

Brain health can be further nurtured simply by being socially active and interacting with others. The more social connections an individual has, and the more bonding they do, the happier they tend to feel. Socializing improves mood and sends a signal to the brain to release the feel-good hormone, oxytocin, which is believed to intensify the memory. Play chess with friends or debate a storyline at a book club and you'll also develop your analytic and problem-solving skills.

It goes without saying, though, that even if you do your utmost to look after your gray matter, your mind and body won't reap any rewards if you're stressed. Anyone with high levels of cortisol, the stress hormone, will struggle to take in new information and retrieve it from their memory. Do what you can to relax. Meditate or practice yoga, anything that will help to slow you down. Screening out everyday distractions will also make you more focused and, therefore, more likely to remember that the car keys are always kept in a kitchen drawer and not randomly left on a work surface somewhere.

After a good night's sleep, attention and concentration levels are more likely to be on top form, so get into the habit of allowing yourself enough time to rest and unwind. Sleep is also necessary for consolidating memories and studies indicate that having 40 winks after learning new information will help you to retain it. A short siesta really is a power nap.

MAKE IT UNFORGETTABLE FUN

From writing lists and posting sticky notes on the fridge to setting reminder alerts for dates and events on your cell phone, everyone has their preferred way to prompt their memory. However, with passwords, PINs, and people's names to remember too, some days you may wish it was all a little easier. Thankfully, it can be. With the help of a few mnemonic aids (see below), you can learn clever and amusing techniques that will train your brain to better encode, store, and recall important information.

1 Concoct a rhyme

There's a bill to pay on the first of the month and you're wondering if that day is fast approaching, do you resort to reciting a rhyme? Thirty days hath September, April, June, and November—it's amazing how this handy poem, probably learned a long time ago, comes quickly to mind. But what about remembering the names of the new couple who have moved into the house opposite? It may be easier if you can come up with a little ditty, along the lines of "Joe and Sue are now living at number two." Try making up a rhyme to nudge your memory. It can be entertaining.

2 Invent an acronym

ASAP, BYOB, AWOL, LOL—abbreviations and acronyms are commonplace in today's world, and not only do they make texting a lot quicker, they can also be a great aid when it comes to remembering lists. For example, you need to go to the grocery store for water, oranges, milk, bacon, an avocado, and tofu. If you think of a WOMBAT rather than six individual items, you're less likely to forget anything. Worried you'll miss your cut and blow-dry on Thursday? Spend the early part of the week imagining yourself wearing a HAT (Hairdresser, Appointment, Thursday) and the booking shouldn't slip your memory.

3 Focus on a face

Creating a visual image that links a person's name to something distinctive about their face can prevent a dreaded blank mind during introductions. If Paul is tall and Lynn is thin, then hooray, you've found an easy association. As for Florence, perhaps if she has pink healthy cheeks, you can remember her as Flo with the rosy glow. Another option is to use alliteration and pick up on something that makes a person stand out, for example, Canadian Carl or Pug-loving Polly. It's not always wise though to share your memory tool, especially if you've come to know your neighbor as Gossip Gloria.

4 Divide into chunks

When you're given a string of numbers, maybe a telephone number, and you can't take a photo or note it on a piece of paper, it's much easier to remember if you break it down into sections. Take each of these chunks and think of something meaningful you can link the number to, an important date or possibly a favorite song. For example, you see an electrician's truck and want to memorize his contact details, 01264 871945. You could just repeat it over and over again, but it's simpler to chunk it into smaller parts—the first three digits are in order (012), The Beatles released *When I'm Sixty-Four* (64) and *Eight Days A Week* (87), and World War Two ended in 1945. Better still, relate the numbers back to you: You were born on April 6, your grandchildren are aged eight and seven, your zip code includes the number 19, and so on.

5 Tell a story

Worried you'll forget where you parked the car in the parking lot? If you don't have a pen to jot down Floor 4, Row C, Space 11, you risk getting lost after some retail therapy. Making up a story in your mind about an adventure where you're scrambling along the floor on all fours, then rowing across the sea (think C), before being propelled into space aboard Apollo 11, might just help.

Storytelling works for passwords, too. Building a mental tale through images can help make a string of numbers and/or letters easier to recall. For example, the password "NY25ccW35S" could be related to a New York (NY) trip you took around Christmas time (Dec 25) when you enjoyed cosmopolitan cocktails while staying in a hotel on West 35th Street (W35S). Use your imagination and have fun.

A place to be

Time spent somewhere cherished—even if it's just for a few hours—can be a perfect opportunity to refresh and re-energise

Certain places hold unique meaning. It could be a hillside with a winding path, a stretch of sandy beach, even a bustling restaurant. The location isn't important. It's a spot that has a particular connection and always seems to make you feel grounded, relaxed, and happy. And often it's places right on your doorstep—a bench in a busy urban square, a local library—that offer the greatest sense of joy.

That hillside walk, for example, might be special because its views never fail to bring you to a standstill or it could be it recalls heartfelt childhood memories. A return to the same hillside or forest walk can be uplifting and help to clear the mind. As the essayist, poet, philosopher, and civil liberties advocate Henry David Thoreau wrote: "Heaven is under our feet as well as over our heads." There's also the fact that being outside can help to improve sleep, boost levels of vitamin D, and strengthen the immune system. Additionally, a walk in nature is an opportunity to keep in touch with everyday beauty, something that's often taken for granted, and an activity that can be done alone or with friends.

Others might find meaning and pleasure in a bookstore or gallery. The act of browsing books or taking time to reflect on a painting can provide breathing space as well as a chance to nurture the soul. The important thing is to find a place that has personal significance or brings joy. A local café could be a go-to spot—and not just because it guarantees a great cup of coffee. It might also feel special because of the easy way you can chat to the owner or barista about everyday life. It can feel good to be a regular whether it's at the local café, a small grocery store, or the community library. Once inside, there's commonly a warm welcome and a friendly smile.

Nostalgia can play a big part in why a location might be treasured. For instance, a stroll along a seaside promenade where your partner first declared their love for you could bring back happy memories of that day. You may also be reminded of the continued strength of those feelings strolling hand-in-hand on a return trip. This is the case for photographer and filmmaker Clive Booth. In 2008, he married his partner, Mari, in Portmeirion in Gwynedd, Wales, and the couple regularly return to the area.

"We usually visit out of season and as soon as we go through the gates and see the hydrangea bushes devoid of color, we get a sense of anticipation," reveals Clive. "The location and geography of the place, the buildings, trees, hills, and water are all pleasing to the eye. But it's more than that. Once I'm there, I feel calm, safe, secure—almost like I've entered a dream state and have escaped the world. Yet as well as feeling calm, I also feel invigorated and reenergized."

Clive recognizes it's a place of huge emotional significance for him. As well as it being where he and Mari were married there are other personal connections. "It's also somewhere we've visited with family and friends, some of whom have gone now. I remember walking down the beach with Mari and close family, just as the sun was setting, and thinking: 'This won't happen again.' In that moment, I felt happy and sad. Talking to members of my family after the loss of Mari's dad, I realized the significance of that time together, when they [also] shared how happy they were to have been there that day. It's a magical place that tugs at your head and your heart."

The best thing is that a special place doesn't even have to involve leaving home. It could be sitting in a cozy chair expertly positioned to listen to a favorite piece of music, sipping a glass of wine on a balcony with rooftop views, or relaxing in a gently scented bubble-filled bath. Close the front door, relax, and enjoy your special place.

TODAY, IF I HAD THE CHANCE, I'D GO TO. . .

What's on your doorstep? Is there a café you regularly visit, a bench where you sit and people-watch, or a gallery where you love to go? Is there a place you've kept secret to try to prevent it becoming overcrowded? Try not to think too much about it—go with first reactions. And remember it can be home or away. Now think about how and why it's special or offers welcome breathing space:

What feelings arise when you think about this place?

Is it somewhere you prefer to be alone or with others?

Does it remind you of a particular time?

Does it remind you of friends or family?

Does it calm your mind?

Do you smile when you think of being there?

How safe does being there make you feel?

Do thoughts feel less crowded while you're there?

Do you feel refreshed or lighter when you come away?

Moving on up

Are you considering uprooting for pastures new? Plan ahead to make sure the move is a seamless (maybe even enjoyable) experience

Moving home is often cited as one of life's most stressful events, but it can also be extremely exciting, especially if it heralds the start of a new chapter. Maybe the move is to the location of your dreams, to bring you closer to cherished family and friends, or to allow you to indulge more freely in a much-loved pastime. Whatever the reason, there's no need for your health and well-being to suffer. In fact, a move might be just what's needed to put a spring back in your step.

When family eventually leave the nest, and there's no longer the constraints to live near a particular school or workplace, other opportunities arise. Do you long to wake up and open the curtains to see the sea, rolling fields, or a vibrant cityscape? If so, then you could make it happen. You could choose to be in a rural spot with a wealth of scenic walks on your doorstep, or a culturally diverse town center where you'll be spoiled for choice when it comes to evening entertainment. Close your eyes and imagine yourself there. It's tempting, isn't it?

Mention a move to family and friends, though, and more often than not, they'll think you're downsizing. And, while that may be a desire for some, it's not for everyone and it isn't essential. Just because you live with only one other person, or on your own, it doesn't automatically follow that you want to eat in a tiny kitchen or have your treasured belongings cramped into a small living room. On the contrary, you might be looking for an extra room that can house an art studio or craft workshop, or you might feel you finally have the time you've always longed for to look after a bigger garden.

If you're moving from an expensive city location, relocating somewhere a little more remote may allow you to buy a similar or notably bigger property. And if the mortgage is paid, or the end is not far off, then any money left over (after costs, of course) could be spent on home improvements, vacations, or hobbies.

Decisions, decisions, decisions

Whether you're relocating to another part of the country or moving to a new home in your current area, there are plenty of considerations. Upping sticks and settling somewhere you love, but not a place in which you've spent a significant amount of time, carries risks. A charming town by the sea can be a wonderful destination for a few weeks in the summer, but it'll have a different vibe during winter months when cafés close and bus services are reduced. To be truly confident a move is the right decision, it's worth renting a property in a new spot first before making a firm commitment to buy. Not being in a chain will also mean that when you do come to make an offer, you'll be seen as a more attractive buyer.

Another way to avoid the potential problems of being in a chain is to buy a new-build. These properties come with a builder's warranty, so you shouldn't be faced with any wildly expensive maintenance bills that older buildings can suddenly spring on you. This type of home should be more energy efficient, too.

Wherever you decide to put down new roots, and whichever type of property becomes your new home-sweet-home, don't underestimate the hold your old home is likely to retain on your heart. Many happy days and key events will have been spent under its roof—anniversaries celebrated, challenges conquered, and, most likely, tears shed. Memories abound within the walls, so any move will be emotional. Take stock, however, and remind yourself that exciting new adventures await. The next instalment of your life is about to begin—and everyone knows sequels are often better.

SMOOTH MOVES

Here are some top tips to help ease the transition from your old home to your new life. . .

Write a wish list

If you're still unsure where you really want to be, start compiling a wish list of criteria. Do you want your new home to be within easy striking distance of public transport? Are you keen to be close to a grocery store, restaurant, or golf course? Is a sea view something you long for? If you no longer want your daily dog walks to involve getting in a car, are there plenty of places to roam nearby? Of course, your needs are likely to change over the next 10 or 20 years, so it can be an idea to factor that in, too. The same goes for the type of home you want. How many spare bedrooms do you need for visitors? If grandchildren sleep over only six times a year, would a sofa bed make more sense, so you can free up a room for, say, a sewing machine? List your priorities and try to stick to them when home-hunting.

Declutter

When you know a move is on the horizon, get ahead by starting to declutter. First-time home owners rarely have more than a few boxes of belongings, but as the years pass, homes fill up. It's amazing what you can accumulate. Travel souvenirs, sports equipment, clothes that either no longer suit or fit—regardless of the size of property you're moving to, go through all your stuff and decide what to sell, donate to a local thrift store, or put in a box destined for the recycling center. Take your time, though, as memories will come flooding back. Enjoy the nostalgic experience and take photographs of items you are struggling to offload if they hold sentimental value for you.

Ask for help

Even if you've single-handedly run a successful business, when it comes to moving home, get as much help as you can. It's not a slight on your organizational capabilities. Ask a friend to look after the cat, get family to help with garden chores, and consider using a professional removal company. Leave the experts to pack fragile items and lift heavy furniture. On the day of the move, important documents and valuable or sentimental items should travel with you.

Say your goodbyes

An older neighbor, your yoga instructor, the owner of your favorite café—you may be surprised at the number of people you miss (and who miss you) when you move home. It doesn't have to mean the end of friendships, however. Keeping in touch is easy, thanks to social media, emails, and cell phones. Friends might also welcome an invitation to pay you a visit in your new home. There's no need to rush any goodbyes. Make sure you find time to spend with the people you've connected to and care about. Visit places that are dear to you as well.

Acknowledge any losses

Moving home is a life-changing event, and amid all the packed boxes, there'll no doubt be a moment when reality strikes and the enormity of the situation hits you. Life is moving on, too. Once-dependent sons and daughters have set up their own homes, business suits now gather dust at the back of the wardrobe—this is a new chapter and while the world is your oyster, the unknown can be daunting. It's okay to feel sad, apprehensive, and a sensation of loss. Appreciate what you've had, be proud of your achievements, and thank your home for being a safe haven where many wonderful memories were made. Only when you acknowledge what you're leaving behind will you be able to fully benefit from the fresh start ahead.

Look after yourself

There's no doubt that moving home can be stressful, but if you accept it's only a temporary situation, then you'll be able to see the light at the end of the tunnel. Some elements will be out of your control, so try not to worry about them. Instead, remain calm and focus your energy on productive matters that you can take care of, such as finding a new doctor, and switching broadband suppliers. Have a few early nights before the day of the move and maintain a healthy diet—you'll then arrive at your new home feeling on top form.

Settle in slowly

Don't arrive at your new address and try to make changes all at once. Okay, so the bathroom needs decorating, but give yourself a chance to settle in before you start opening every paint can. After a few weeks, you may realize that the south-facing room destined to be your dining space works better as a reading room. The same rule applies with the garden. Don't be super keen to start redesigning an area. First and foremost, get acquainted with your new home. It's a new relationship, after all.

GET SMART

With technology fast moving into every corner of the home as well as the office, how can it improve well-being and make everyday tasks that bit easier?

Open any paper, listen to a radio show, or watch TV right now and the chances are it won't be long before you hear the term "Smart Home." It's bandied about as though anyone who knows anything about technology will be fully conversant with what it is and what it means. Yet even the most IT literate of folk—who've been using PCs since the year dot, were early adopters of online banking, and embrace smartphone apps—might have missed out on aspects of the smart home revolution. It's unsurprising, really, given the speed and scale of the changes, yet this new category of technology opens up the means of easier living within the home.

The most straightforward benefit of smart tech is remote control. Regular remote control has been around for years, with the likes of TVs, DVDs, and CDs, but wireless smart-home networking systems that require no daily charging have taken it to a new level. Need to turn on or adjust your heating without leaving your couch (or the room for that matter)? Check. Want to switch on the hall lights without getting out of bed? Check. Want to make sure the stove hasn't been left on after you've gone out for the evening? Check. With an internet-enabled device to hand, sometimes all you need do is say the word—you don't even always have to press a button any more (devices that do still require the touch of a button often have accessibility modes and are available in large sizes). The upshot is that it puts you in control and, in some instances, can make it easier to reside for longer in your own home.

Voice control

Voice-activated requests, where you ask a machine to perform a task rather than tapping or swiping a smartphone or a tablet, offer the immediate benefit of distance. You no longer have to be in the same room as those TVs or DVD players mentioned earlier. This long-distance remote control is still just a control, though,

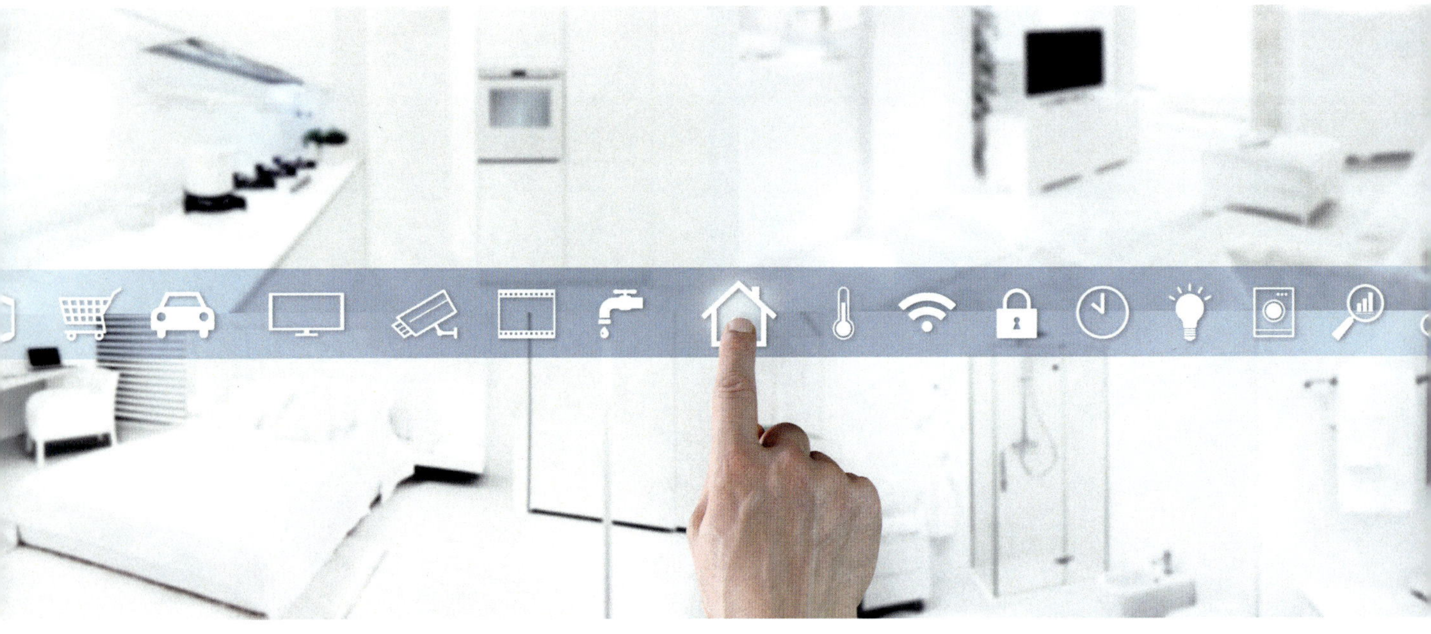

albeit one activated in a clever way. It isn't really where the "smart" comes from—that stems from sensors, which can be connected to the network and, crucially, software that can take input from them. In practical terms, this means a heating system that can warm the house before you get home, lights that flash a certain color at a set time, perhaps as a reminder to take medication, and alerts that indicate if someone has fallen over and needs help.

Certain devices are also better able to cooperate via the internet, such as modern smoke detectors from eco-system firm Nest, which rather than emit a piercing alarm, will give clear voice instructions, switch on lights, and, if programmed to do so, notify a relative of the situation via an app.

Smartphones and tablets are crucial parts of any smart home, but there are other means of communication. Smart speakers, for instance, can be spoken to without a phone. In use, simply saying the "wake word," followed by a query or simple command, for example, "Alexa, what time is it?", can achieve a lot. At the moment, none of the voice-activated control systems is perfect. Some think they've heard their wake words when they haven't (or they've misheard something from a TV or radio), which can be annoying for even the most technically sophisticated. The clipped manner of successful exchanges can be quite frustrating, too. The technology, however, is improving by the day and being promoted for everyone—having smart speakers in the corner of a room is standard in many modern homes.

One of the particularly nice things about these devices is that they can be used to make calls to loved ones without the need for handsets. The Google Home Hub and Amazon Echo Show also boast screens, so they can be used for visual calls—again without the need for a handheld device.

Physical health

Another fast-growing area of smart tech is wearables—this is especially true in the worlds of fitness and medicine. These products can help you collect information about your health that can be used for self-improvement or given to your doctor. Other everyday devices, such as smart scales, can track muscle mass and body fat as well as weight, all of which helps to explore and analyze any weight gain. In all these cases, a smartphone or tablet is once again the key. Stepping on the scales every day is easy, but keeping a log of all these stats is where the benefit lies, and is a lot more likely to happen if it's done automatically.

Emerging technologies are changing the landscape, but as with any market, the desire to capitalize on the needs of older people has also led to some products that fall short of the mark, so make sure anything you buy is fully tried-and-tested. Technology is only as smart as the innovators deploying it, and they're not all thinking about the consumer, or even treating the problem humanely.

"Aging is often framed as a problem technology can solve, and older people are positioned as lonely and disengaged," says Amanda Lazar, assistant professor at the University of Maryland. Perhaps rather than creating products on the basis of perceived defects, more success will come from researching what older people actually want. Take the company LiliSmart—it offers a smart watch with a simple screen for the older user that can give medication and meal reminders, track location, and, yes, detect falls. This information is sent to a loved one or caregiver (who are also customers) via smartphone alerts. It's not too intrusive and, while it can't prevent falls, it can help to ensure they're followed up.

There has also been increased integration of functions like fall-detection into existing devices including the

Apple Watch. When it detects a fall followed by motionlessness, it warns that a fall was detected and, if there is no response, summons the emergency services. If you're over 65 when you first set up your Apple Watch, this feature is automatically enabled.

Mental health

What can technology do to help tackle dementia or loneliness? Some think the effects of dementia can be eased by enabling those with the condition to continue to perform as many everyday tasks as possible without outside help. Smart tech might have a role to play here. Smart sensors, for instance, detect dangers, while smart ovens can switch themselves off if they've been left on for too long. This supports a person's desire to stay in their home while helping to promote self-confidence.

Smart tech can also alert caregivers of worrying situations. A smartphone's live GPS location sensor (if enabled) can indicate that a relative who has dementia has strayed outside a designated safe zone.

For those who are indoors more than they would like and are, therefore, exposed to more artificial light, there are products that mimic some of the positive effects of being outdoors.

Artificial light, for example, stays exactly the same color temperature all day whereas outdoors the sun rises with a bluish tone and becomes pure white at midday, before getting warmer in the evening. This can have a positive effect on people's health and well-being. One of the firms to offer a solution is Philips Hue. Its smart ambience lights can be programmed to match the time of day and the tone is adjustable via an app.

What's next?

The near future is likely to be about more and better software at both the practical level (sensors building up data from users to reduce the number of false-positives) and the system level (better integration of monitoring and communications systems). This is true of all smart tech, not just that aimed at age-specific markets.

There are now clear standards required to work with Apple or Google or Amazon Alexa systems, and with so many smart speakers and smartphones out there it's in manufacturers' interests to meet them.

In the more distant future, greater connectivity and more sensors will make it possible to take the protection out of the home. The Smart Cambridge pilot scheme in the UK is a plan to integrate sensors so, for example, sidewalk sensors warn of ice (currently the cause of 3,000 falls a year in the UK). But the scheme is even more ambitious and aims to integrate all the data sources in the city—traffic, parking, bus positions, air quality, weather, waste, and more—and make it available not just to the city for live management and policy planning, but also to third-party developers to create information apps.

Imagine the same thing on a smaller scale—a single app that securely unites people and their caregivers so both can access and share information about movement and heart rates gleaned from all the individual devices securely connected to it. Privacy would remain paramount but the smart tech could enable many to live a safer, more confident life in their own home.

FIVE THINGS SMART TECH CAN DO NOW

Internet-connected cameras
Cameras that connect to the internet provide security (like any CCTV system), but they can also be used by the family or a caregiver to check in and initiate a two-way conversation thanks to built-in speakers.

Household emergency sensors
As well as traditional presence and door sensors, which you might find in a standard burglar alarm, leak sensors can be fitted under sinks so any plumbing disasters can be sensed and nipped in the bud before problems arise.

Smart doorbells
A doorbell with a remote display on the user's phone or tablet gives the homeowner a chance to stop the mailman turning away with your delivery before you make it to the door.

Pill reminders
Apps like Medisafe can buzz a smartphone or wristwatch with pill reminders, while some devices, including Pivotell Advance, can text up to three people if pills aren't taken.

Apps
Most smartphones include a pedometer or step counter. Keeping an eye on activity in retirement is a great way to stave off more serious health problems in the long run—and the chances are most people already have this feature on their device.

STRIKE A *pose*

Why golden yoga might be for you

Middle-class, white, skinny, female—yoga has a reputation, which is a shame as it couldn't be any further from what this ancient practice is all about. (That said, however, the above description pretty much sums me up and I've been in the yoga world for almost 20 years.)

Now, taking a closer look at yoga from an outside perspective, I can't help but wonder if clever marketing, fitness fashions, and a little luck (depending on your perspective) helped to steer yoga toward this narrow, deep-pocketed demographic and away from those who didn't fit the brief, and that includes anyone whose age looked like it might just begin with a five, let alone a six, seven, or eight.

Yes, there are forms of yoga that require a huge amount of stamina, strength, and as little clothing as possible, but they are far from the true lineage of this ancient, healing practice. And knowing all its benefits, I'm confident that this is the practice I will take with me into my golden years.

If you're interested in yoga but, deterred by the stereotype, haven't yet dared to cross the threshold, perhaps these few benefits here will encourage you to try it. . .

Body and mind connection The body changes. At various points people are less strong, supple, or able as they once were. Yoga brings you into your body and helps you to have a strong appreciation for it "as it is now" and for all that is has done and still does for you.

Your body is your home for the duration of life. Whatever its age and strengths and weaknesses, it's a wonderful gift. Yoga is designed to honor, respect, and appreciate the body through physical practices, breath work, and meditation. I know of no other activity that addresses these ideals in the same way.

Flexibility Tightness and inflexibility is not only limited to the limbs, hips, and external parts of the body. Chances are if a person is inflexible on the outside they are also inflexible on the inside. Medical science suggests there might be a correlation with a tight chest and tight arteries, which can be a contributory factor in poor heart health. A flexible body is one where all systems are flowing.

Think of your body as a circuit board. It isn't just blood, lymph, and hormones that circulate—the body is an energetic system constantly recycling energy, thoughts, messages, and emotions. If you are tight, then this vital life force energy can get stuck. Even 10 minutes of stretching a day can have a huge impact on your body's flexibility and will allow everything to circulate. Picture a flowing river instead of a stagnant pond. You may not be doing shoulderstands (see left) right away, but in time you'll be stretching more than you thought.

Mobility Exercise and movement is vital at any age, but perhaps more so if you wish to continue to have an active lifestyle. Walking is great, but it doesn't work so much on strengthening and stretching the muscles in the back, shoulders, arms, and core. Yoga applies to the whole body. There are hundreds of different poses and it can help to ensure that all parts of the body remain mobile, which will allow practitioners to continue to lead a more active life than they would otherwise enjoy.

Pain management My personal goal for yoga and the future is to remain pain free. As someone who has suffered chronic back pain after the births of three large babies, I have felt the isolation and hopelessness of waking up in pain every day. Yoga is not a quick fix and most of the benefits happen as a culmination of a lot of practice. Once a balanced, flexible, and strong body has been achieved, a regular yoga practice can help to maintain a pain-free existence.

Sense of purpose and belonging Yoga is a community. A community is one with people of all ages and walks of life and in the past, it has been a concern that yoga has drawn from a narrow demographic. This is changing. We all have so much to learn from one another. I learn from people older than me and I also learn so much and am so inspired by people younger than me. My yoga community is really important as we meet together to do something wonderful for ourselves. We share a common interest in self-care, being the best we can be, contributing and being in service. Being part of a community of people who are facing their edges and their fears and who all have a common goal is a wonderful thing.

Mental health Facing the latter stages rather than the beginning or middle of one's life can be daunting. When the time comes that the body is ready to go, it is then—if we have had the privilege of a long life—that we will face our true spiritual beliefs. Whether this is related to religion or not, it is faith that will sustain us. Yoga is a practice that brings you into the moment. It is a practice that unites you with your spirit—the part of you that isn't your body, that doesn't age, and that will never die. Yoga itself connects body and mind through mindful movement. When that movement is not accessible, it is still possible to practice meditation, connection, and breath.

Ultimately yoga is a spiritual practice. Within it is a sequence of postures called the warrior poses. This is because yoga is the warriors' path and it takes courage and strength to meet oneself in this stripped-back way. If you decide to take a step onto this path, away from today's over-stimulated world, at some point you will meet yourself. That's when you will really start to open and heal. And that's something we can all do.

TIPS FOR BEGINNERS

If you're approaching yoga in your senior years, seek out a beginners' hatha yoga class or a beginners' Iyengar class. Avoid hot yoga, vinyasa yoga, and anything with "power" in the title.

Try a few different classes until you find a teacher with whom you click. He or she will be happy to talk to you about your options and what might work for you.

Yes, you might be the oldest person in the class, the most inflexible, or the one needing the most assistance (at first), but we are never too young or old to be students.

With regular practice, you'll soon make steady improvements, whether that's physically, emotionally, or mentally.

Yoga is not a competitive sport and a good teacher will have set up a safe learning environment where effort, not results, are praised and everyone in the room is comfortable and confident in their own ability and not comparing themselves to anyone.

Remember, if you look around the room, that even the most seemingly "good" person is probably dealing with their own insecurities.

Words: **Michelle Moroney**
Michelle is a senior yoga teacher, certified Health and Wellness Coach, and runs her own retreat center, the Cliffs of Moher Retreat on the West Coast of Ireland. She is passionate about helping people to take ownership of their complete health—body, mind, and higher self. She dons her health coaching hat in her role as retreat manager and has created a range of programs, offering a variety of experiences to inspire and educate.

STRETCH OUT

*If you're new to yoga, here are a few postures to try at home. . .**

MOUNTAIN POSE (*Tadasana*)

- Stand with feet hip-width apart, toes pointing forward.
- Ground the body through the feet, but avoid "collapsing."
- Visualize a thread passing through the body and up through the crown of your head.
- Aim for a gentle elongation from the waist up.
- Relax and take five even breaths.

Alternative option

Sitting on a chair, take a deep breath and sit up straight, extending your spine. As you exhale, root down into the chair with your sit bones. Your legs should be at 90-degree angles, knees directly over your ankles. There should be a little room between the knees. Take a deep breath and, as you exhale, roll your shoulders down your back, pull your bellybutton in toward your spine, and relax your arms down at your sides. If possible, lift your toes and press firmly into all four corners of the feet. Relax and take five even breaths.

FORWARD FOLD (*Uttanasana*)

- From *Tadasana*, exhale, fold forward from the hip joint, and lengthen through the spine (pelvis tips forward). Bend your knees as necessary to feel comfortable and safe in your lower back.
- Your hands can go to the shins, or the ground in front of you, or beside your feet—wherever feels comfortable.
- Press heels into the ground and lift your sit bones up.
- Inhale, lengthen through your spine to the tip of your crown, exhale, and fold a little more. Broaden through the collarbones, gaze to your shins.
- If it feels comfortable and stable, take a hold of the opposite elbows and dangle down.
- When ready, inhale as you lift your torso back into an upright position.

Alternative option

If you have difficulty with balance, try *Paschimottanasana* (seated forward bend).

From a seated position, focus on lengthening the spine and neck, and with the hands on the knees hinge forward from the hips. Bend your knees as necessary to feel comfortable. Once forward, allow the head to relax down. (Anyone with arthritis or a spinal condition needs to use caution when relaxing the head down. In this case it might be preferable to keep the head up.) Take five even breaths. Inhale as you lift your torso back into an upright position.

SITTING SIDE BEND (*Parsva sukhasana*)

- From a seated position on the floor, legs straight, place your right hand under your right buttock and draw the flesh out to the side. Repeat with your left buttock.
- Sit up tall onto your sit bones (the lowest part of your tailbone, or the two points that take the weight when you sit).
- Cross your legs at the shins and place your feet under your knees, flex your feet (effectively, sit cross-legged). With both hands hold your right upper thigh and gently roll the flesh outward, repeat with your left thigh.
- "Walk" the fingertips of your right hand sideways away from your hip until they come to a point that is comfortable. Inhale and lift your left arm above you, then bend to the right (you will feel a stretch on your left-hand side).
- Bring the fingertips of your left hand behind your ear as you bend deeper.
- Relax and take five even breaths. When ready, inhale as you lift your torso back into an upright position.
- Repeat the posture on the opposite side of the body.

LOCUST (*Shalabhasana*)

- Lie on your front, arms by your sides, palms facing your body, forehead resting on the ground.
- Inhale, press into your pubic bone, lift your head, upper torso, arms, and legs, lift with the whole back.
- Reach your chest forward and up, extend your arms toward your feet, lift your legs up, and press through the balls of your feet, roll your inner thighs up.
- Broaden through the collarbones, firm your shoulder blades, keep the neck long, and gaze slightly forward.
- Take five even breaths. When ready, lower the body to face the floor once more.

** If you have any concerns about your health or are unwell, have injuries, or any ongoing physical symptoms such as back or knee pain, it is strongly advised that you visit your doctor before embarking on a course of yoga or attempting any postures, especially without a qualified instructor. Only stretch your body to the point where it is comfortable. If you feel discomfort or pain in any of the postures, discontinue and slowly return to a position that is comfortable.*

Please note: the yoga pictures shown have been used for illustrative purposes only and do not necessarily reflect the poses described above.

TREAT YOUR FEET

They're truly a feat of natural engineering, walking you through life while withstanding great stress, which is why these sensitive soles deserve a little extra care. Here's a guide to giving those hard-working feet the love and attention they so richly deserve

Feet are incredibly resilient, capable of balancing a person's entire body weight and carrying them over all kinds of terrain throughout life. On average, a person takes between 8,000 and 10,000 steps a day, which equates to several tons of force on their feet. They really are put through their paces. Feet become longer and wider with age. This is because of a loss of elasticity in the skin, tendons, and ligaments that link each tiny bone. It's not surprising that extra attention is required to ensure feet stay healthy and nimble.

Properly maintaining healthy feet involves checking them on a regular basis to identify any problems. A good time to do this is after a shower or while taking a bath. Look out for dry, cracked, sore, or peeling skin. Are there any corns or calluses? Remember to check the condition of your nails. Is there any discoloration or an ingrowing nail that requires treatment? Keep in mind also that feet are a reflection of your overall health, so if you notice anything unusual—such as recurring loss of sensation, tingling, sore spots, cramping, pain, or discoloration—it's important to have this checked out with a health professional. These regular checks help to ensure that any potential problems are spotted early.

Your feet work hard for you, so take time to treat them as often as you can. Regular warm foot baths can prevent some foot disorders by helping to release tension in the muscles, and there are luxurious foot spas and scrubs (try the homemade recipes on the next page) that will revive and keep feet healthy.

For that extra boost, consider booking an occasional pedicure or reflexology session. When feet are pampered and cared for, it increases feelings of well-being and results in an all-over glow that really does stretch from head to toe.

SELF-CARE FOR HAPPY AND HEALTHY FEET

Foot health practitioner Sara Maguire shares the following routine for keeping your feet healthy. . .

- Immerse your feet into a warm foot bath or foot spa for 10 to 20 minutes and sit back and relax. Use Epsom salts for swollen, tired, and aching feet. My favorite is Gehwol foot salts as they have softening properties and smell beautifully of fresh rosemary and lavender.
- Cut your toenails straight across using a good pair of stainless steel nippers and smooth over the edge of the nail with a file so there are no sharp corners.
- If you have calluses (areas of hard skin), try using soap on a pumice stone or foot file while your feet are immersed in the water, and gently scrub the hard skin to soften and smooth it.
- Dry your feet thoroughly, particularly in-between your toes, as damp, moist skin inter-digitally can lead to painful soft corns and the itchy, uncomfortable fungal skin infection known as athlete's foot.
- Finish off by moisturizing and protecting your skin with a good quality foot cream and heel balm. Look out for creams that have a high content of urea (10-15 percent) as this product rehydrates the skin, can help heal cracks, and prevent the build-up of calluses on your feet when used as part of a daily footcare regime. Massage the cream thoroughly into the feet but take care not to moisturize between the toes or use talcum powder as this can settle, get warm, and lead to the development of athlete's foot. For very dry and cracked heels, put a good quantity of heel balm onto plastic wrap and wrap around your heels. Relax and let it soak in for 20 minutes, remove the film, and then massage any remaining cream into the skin.

HELPING TIRED AND TROUBLED SOLES

Ease dry skin
Feet become less supple as the years pass and skin is prone to dryness, cracks, and splitting. Avoid using harsh soaps or lotions, which can aggravate it. Apply shea butter, which is a rich source of vitamin E as well as being moisturizing and healing. Coconut oil is also an effective antibacterial, antiviral, and antifungal agent, which might help prevent skin infections.

Stay fresh
Massage your feet with a good-quality peppermint foot lotion to revive and freshen them. If you don't have any lotion, you could add a cup of peppermint tea to a bowl of water and soak your feet for 10 minutes.

Treat chilblains
A combination of cold weather and poor circulation is thought to cause chilblains, which often develop on the toes creating patches of red, swollen, and itchy skin. Use calamine lotion or witch hazel to soothe the itching. To prevent chilblains, avoid extremes of temperature. Keep your whole body and feet warm and wear seamless wool socks. Take some gentle exercise to improve circulation to your feet.

Keep fungus away
There are over-the-counter preparations to treat fungal nail or athlete's foot. Tea tree oil is natural and effective. Its antiseptic, antifungal, and antibacterial properties will help combat fungus, which thrives in any warm, moist environment.

Athlete's foot can be treated naturally by soaking your feet in half a cup of apple cider vinegar, two tablespoons of Himalayan salt, and warm water. It's important to completely dry your feet afterward. Seek advice if the problem persists.

Eliminate toxins and dead skin
Every couple of weeks, add a handful of Epsom salts to a bowl of warm water, then soak feet for no longer than 10 to 15 minutes. The action of the salt helps to eliminate toxins from the body via the abundant sweat glands in the feet. This is also a good treat to soften the skin so that any calluses can be gently treated afterward using a pumice stone.

Relax and revive
Suffering from tired feet? Mix three drops of lavender oil, one drop of geranium oil, and one drop of chamomile oil in two teaspoons of olive oil. Massage the blended aromatherapy oils into your feet to relax the muscles and uplift the senses. Once feet are warm, use a foot roller (or a tennis ball) over the soles for several minutes. This releases tension, improves circulation, helps break down toxic deposits, and gives a feeling of a whole body lift.

Investigate sore feet
Might your footwear be the cause of your sore feet? Have your feet measured before buying new shoes. Check for bunions or any structural issues caused by injury or conditions such as arthritis. If soreness continues, consult a foot health specialist.

Treat mind, body, and sole
Gift yourself a reflexology session, which treats the whole person through the feet. This complementary therapy is founded on there being reflex points on each foot, which correspond to organs, structures, and systems within the body. A reflex is when stimulation at one point brings about a response in another. By using pressure techniques on the feet, an experienced practitioner can detect imbalances in the body and these can often be effectively treated to restore well-being.

Best foot forward

TRY OUT A HOMEMADE FOOT BATH AND SCRUB

Honey and lemon foot bath

- Half a cup of honey
- Juice of a whole lemon
- 1 tbsp apple cider vinegar

Fill a bowl with warm water, and add the ingredients. Honey is a natural antibiotic and is full of beneficial antioxidants. Lemon is also rich in antioxidants, and the citric acid can brighten the skin. The apple cider vinegar is antibacterial and contains alpha hydroxy acids, which help remove dead skin. Soak your feet for 10 to 20 minutes and pat them dry. This is a soothing, zesty treat for tired feet.

Rosemary and peppermint foot scrub

- 2 tbsp olive oil
- 1 tsp coconut oil
- 3 drops peppermint essential oil
- 1 drop rosemary essential oil or 1 tsp dried rosemary
- 1 tbsp sea salt

Mix the ingredients together in a small bowl until you have a scrub lotion. Wash your feet and then use the mixture to gently scrub them to deep-cleanse and revitalize. Rosemary is naturally antiseptic and helps protect the skin. It's also claimed to enhance memory and concentration. Peppermint has astringent, antiseptic, and antiinflammatory properties. Gently wipe away the excess and let your feet breathe. Enjoy the refreshing aroma.

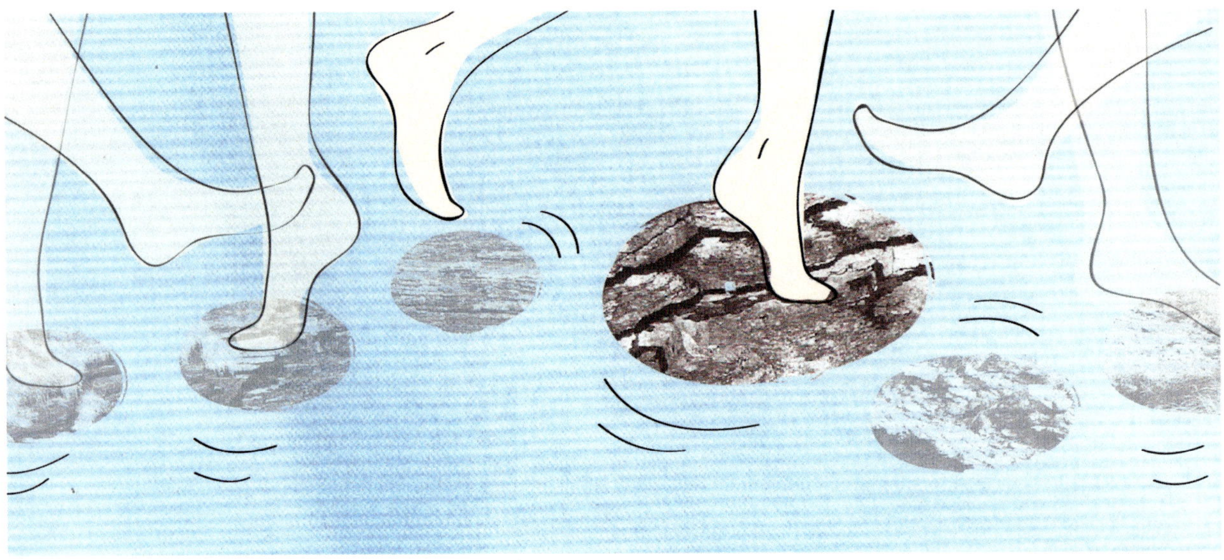

Everyday risks

I'll be honest: I don't like taking risks. I enjoy being in my comfort zone—a place where I know what's going to happen, and how it will pan out. When I try new things, I usually research and plan, plot a course through the unknown, load my dice to ensure the outcome I predict.

I'm not the only one—many people, especially as they get older, avoid risk. It's because risk can prompt fear and anxiety, activated through the brain's stress response. It warns of potential danger, and advises avoiding it at all costs.

If a person has a history of running into stressful situations, the brain can react by going into overdrive—telling them they're in danger even when they're safe at home. Whatever your history, the older you get, the more risk you avoid.

Yet—ironically—removing risk is risky in itself, because the longer you stay cocooned in your own comfort zone, the narrower its walls become. Your "risk threshold" becomes lower year on year, activating your stress response at less and less. And so although I enjoy the familiar, I've been forced to recognize that removing risk from my life isn't wise, and that taking small, manageable risks is beneficial for my brain.

Stepping outside the comfort zone increases the synaptic potential of your neurons. The brain sparks alive the more new, healthy information it has to process—and the more uncomfortable the information, the more connections those neurons make. A flexible brain fizzes with synaptic sparks, making it more adaptable to unfamiliar situations and in an upward cycle, better able to cope with risk.

To do this, you have to find the median point, by taking a risk that doesn't activate stress. It should push your brain out of its well-worn grooves, but without cranking anxiety. If it does, wind it down with a focus on calm, instead of giving in by never taking a chance again.

I've started taking small, everyday risks, nudging myself into unfamiliar territory. Everyone has different definitions of what constitutes a risk. Below, however, is an easy way to lead yourself away from the usual and toward a healthier, more flexible brain, no matter the boundaries of your comfort zone.

STEP BY STEP TO AN EVERYDAY RISK

You are going to take a short, yet unfamiliar journey close to home.

- If you've never caught the bus, take a bus. If you have, choose a different route.
- Plan the journey as briefly as you can—but, of course, ensure you can get home.
- If you start to feel anxious, breathe slowly and deeply. Feeling slightly uncomfortable is good, fearful is bad.
- Attempt to relish each moment of the journey, however short it may be.

Made in United States
Orlando, FL
08 August 2023

35818189R00055